Ephesians
Discipleship Lessons

and Bible Study Commentary for Personal Devotional Use, Small Groups or
Sunday School Classes, and Sermon Preparation for Pastors and Teachers

JesusWalk® Bible Study Series
by Dr. Ralph F. Wilson
Director, Joyful Heart Renewal Ministries

Additional books, and reprint licenses are available at:
http://www.jesuswalk.com/books/ephesians.htm

Free Participant Guide handout sheets are available at:
http://www.jesuswalk.com/ephesians/ephesians-lesson-handouts.pdf

JesusWalk® Publications
Loomis, California

Paperback
ISBN-13: 978-0-9832310-8-0
ISBN-10: 0983231087

Library of Congress Control Number: 2011916167

Library of Congress subject headings:
Bible. – N.T. – Ephesians – Commentaries.

Suggested Classifications
Dewey Decimal System: 227.5
Library of Congress: BS 2695

Published by JesusWalk® Publications, P.O. Box 565, Loomis, CA 95650-0565, USA.

JesusWalk is a registered trademark and Joyful Heart is a trademark of Joyful Heart Renewal Ministries.

Unless otherwise noted, all the Bible verses quoted are from the New International Version (International Bible Society, 1973, 1978), used by permission.

110906

Preface

Of all of St. Paul's Epistles, for me the Letter to the Ephesians is his masterpiece. Though written from prison in Rome, the first half of the Letter is full of praise and worship, an exalted understanding of Christ, and a transcendent view of the Church. He challenges us to leave our lowest selves and inspires us to seek our highest potential in Jesus, seated with him at the right hand of the Father. Here is salvation by grace through faith, as well as the unity and mission of the church. Paul's prayers are amazing in their breadth and scope!

The second half turns from doctrine to application. He spells out what unity looks like and how gifted ministry functions in the church body. Paul's condemnation of sinful attachments is matched by his conviction that the power of Christ can free us to become like "light in the Lord." He paints a portrait of a loving Christian marriage between believing spouses, and compares it to Christ and his Church. This prison epistle concludes with a challenge to "put on the whole armor of God" and to struggle in prayer for victory. All in all, it is an uplifting, glorious epistle, indeed!

Rembrandt, "St. Paul in Prison" (1627), oil on wood, 72.8 x 60.2 cm., Stuttgart, Staatsgalerie. His body may be in prison, but you can see in his face a contemplation of the heavenly realms that he opens for us in Ephesians 1.

The study consists of 16 lessons, eight on the first three chapters and eight on the final three chapters. I hope you enjoy studying Paul's letter to the Ephesians as much as I have.

Dr. Ralph F. Wilson
Loomis, California
October 4, 2006

Table of Contents

Reprint Guidelines

Copying the Handouts. In some cases, small groups or Sunday school classes would like to use these notes to study this material. That's great.

If you're working with a class or small group, feel free to duplicate the following handouts from the appendix at no additional charge. If you'd like to print 8-1/2" x 11" sheets, you can download the free Participant Guide handout sheets at: www.jesuswalk.com/ephesians/ephesians-lesson-handouts.pdf

All charts and notes are copyrighted and must bear the line:

"Copyright © 2011, Ralph F. Wilson. All rights reserved. Reprinted by permission."

You may not resell these notes to other groups or individuals outside your congregation. You may, however, charge people in your group enough to cover your copying costs.

Copying the book (or the majority of it) in your congregation or group, you are requested to purchase a reprint license for each book. A Reprint License, $2.50 for each copy is available for purchase at

www.jesuswalk.com/books/ephesians.htm

Or you may send a check to:

Dr. Ralph F. Wilson
JesusWalk Publications
PO Box 565
Loomis, CA 95650, USA

The Scripture says,

"The laborer is worthy of his hire" (Luke 10:7) and "Anyone who receives instruction in the word must share all good things with his instructor" (Galatians 6:6).

However, if you are from a third world country or an area where it is difficult to transmit money, please make a small contribution instead to help the poor in your community.

References and Abbreviations

Barth   Marcus Barth, *Ephesians 1-3* and *Ephesians 4-6* (Anchor Bible 34 and 34A; Doubleday, 1974)

BDAG   *A Greek-English Lexicon of the New Testament and Other Early Christian Literature*, by Walter Bauer and Frederick William Danker, (Third Edition; based on previous English editions by W.F. Arndt, F.W. Gingrich, and F.W. Danker; University of Chicago Press, 1957, 1979, 2000)

Bruce   F.F. Bruce, *The Epistles to the Colossians, to Philemon, and to the Ephesians* (New International Commentary on the New Testament; Eerdmans, 1984)

DPL   *Dictionary of Paul and His Letters*, edited by Gerald F. Hawthorne, Ralph P. Martin, and Daniel G. Reid (InterVarsity Press, 1993)

Foulkes   Francis Foulkes, *Ephesians* (Second Edition; Tyndale New Testament Commentaries; Eerdmans, 1989)

ISBE   *The International Standard Bible Encyclopedia*, Geoffrey W. Bromiley (general editor), (Eerdmans, 1979-1988; fully revised from the 1915 edition)

KJV   King James Version

Merriam-   *Merriam-Webster's Collegiate Dictionary* (Tenth Edition; Merriam-Webster,
Webster   1993)

NIDNTT   Colin Brown (general editor), *The New International Dictionary of New Testament Theology* (Zondervan, 1975-1978; translated with additions and revisions from *Theologisches Begriffslexikon zum Neuen Testament*, 1967-1971, three volume edition)

NASB   New American Standard Bible (The Lockman Foundation, 1960-1988)

NIV   New International Version (International Bible Society, 1973, 1978)

NJB   New Jerusalem Bible (Darton, Longman & Todd Ltd, 1985)

NRSV   New Revised Standard Version (Division of Christian Education of the National Council of Churches of Christ, USA, 1989)

O'Brien   Peter T. O'Brien, *The Letter to the Ephesians* (The Pillar New Testament Commentary; Eerdmans, 1999)

TDNT   Gerhard Kittel and Gerhard Friedrich (editors), Geoffrey W. Bromiley (translator and editor), *Theological Dictionary of the New Testament* (Eerdmans, 1964-1976; translated from *Theologisches Wörterbuch zum Neuen Testament*, ten volume edition)

Thayer   Joseph Henry Thayer, *Greek-English Lexicon of the New Testament* (Associated Publishers and Authors, n.d., reprinted from 1889 edition)

Introduction to Paul's Letter to the Ephesians

In the estimation of many, Ephesians is Paul's crowning work, "the quintessence of Paulinism."[1] It is both a literary gem and a treasure of spiritual nuggets. Those who study it may not fully plumb its depths, but will glean important understanding of Christ and his Church, as well as lessons for life.

Before we get into the book itself, let's see what we can learn about it.

The amphitheater at Ephesus could seat 24,000 people (Acts 19:29ff)

Authorship

On the surface, authorship may seem self-evident, since the first sentence reads rather clearly: "Paul, an apostle of Christ Jesus by the will of God....." For 18 centuries Paul's authorship was uncontested. But since F.C. Bauer questioned Pauline authorship in 1845, it has become popular in some circles to deny that Paul was the author and speculate about others. In fact, these days the majority of critical scholars deny Pauline authorship for several reasons:

1. **Language**. Ephesians includes a number of words not found in other Pauline letters.
2. **Style**. The first half of the Letter, especially, has a full and lofty style, unlike other Pauline letters.
3. **Theology**. The Letter's view of Christ is cosmic in scope and the author's understanding of the Church, too, is advanced.
4. **Colossians**. Many elements of Ephesians are similar to Colossians, so much that some scholars see "borrowing" from the ideas in Colossians.

[1] Bruce, p. 229.

5. **Personal References**. Unlike Paul's other letters, Ephesians doesn't include greetings to various believers in the church to which he was writing.

Of course, each of these objections can be answered by those who believe Paul to be the author. Paul is a highly educated man, quite able to express himself in different ways, depending upon his knowledge, the revelation he is seeking to express, and the heresies he desires to combat. If you consider the different styles and language usage skilled communicators are capable of today, it's not hard to grant those abilities to Paul. The theology is not discontinuous with other Pauline letters, but builds on them, reflecting growth in understanding that comes from both revelation and theological reflection resulting in a bigger vision of Christ and his church. And as for borrowing from Colossians ... if Paul is the author of both Colossians and Ephesians, the concept of borrowing becomes pretty silly.

There are two very good reasons to see Paul as the author of Ephesians.

1. Tradition. Ephesians was considered authored by Paul from the earliest days of the church, and quoted by the earliest of the Apostolic Fathers – Clement of Rome, Ignatius, Hermas, and Polycarp. Even the non-orthodox acknowledged it as Pauline – Marcion, Gnostic writers, the Nag Hammadi documents, and others. In the early church, Pauline authorship was never once questioned.

2. Autobiographical information. Paul claims to be the author (1:1), and reflects on his "stewardship of the mystery" (3:2-6), the nature of his apostolic ministry (3:7-13), his imprisonment (3:1; 4:1; 6:20), his first-person appeals and prayers for his readers, his request for prayer (6:21-22), and his comments about Tychicus. The literary device of pseudonymity may have been common in the early Christian centuries in some accepted Christian documents, but deliberate deception? Since the author claims to be Paul (1:1; 3:1) and personally solicits the readers' prayers, anyone besides Paul claiming this would be purposely deceiving the readers – hardly worthy of a writer who tells us to "put off falsehood and speak truthfully" to our neighbor (4:25).[2]

---

[2] Those who claim Paul was not the author point to a supposed Christian tradition and literary device of pseudonymity, wherein later works are attributed to great Christian leaders, not as a fiction but a way of honoring them. The truth is that while there were many pseudonymous works in the first several centuries of the church, there are no pseudonymous works in the New Testament canon. The early Fathers were insistent that the New Testament be a record of the apostles' teaching. Donaldson asserts, "No one ever seems to have accepted a document as religiously and philosophically prescriptive which was known to be forged. I do not know a single example" (L.R. Donelson, *Pseudepigraphy and Ethical Argument in the Pastoral Epistles* (Tübigen: J.C.B. Mohr, 1986), p. 11; cited by O'Brien, p. 40).

I believe Paul was the author of Ephesians and am joined by a number of recent scholars, including Marcus Barth (1974), F.F. Bruce (1984), and Peter T. O'Brien (1999). The case for Pauline authorship, in my view, is substantial and convincing, while the case against it is speculative and (except to some scholars) pretty spotty evidence on which to overthrow Apostolic authorship of Ephesians.

Place and Date

Paul founded the church at Ephesus over a period of nearly three years (Acts 19:1-20:1), from about 52 to 55 AD. He visited with the church elders on the beach at Miletus on his way to Jerusalem (Acts 20:17-38). In Jerusalem, Paul was arrested about 57 AD and imprisoned, first in Caesarea (about 57 to 59 AD) and then under house arrest in Rome about 60 to 62 AD. (Acts 28:16-31). He probably died no later than 63 to 65 AD, and probably earlier.

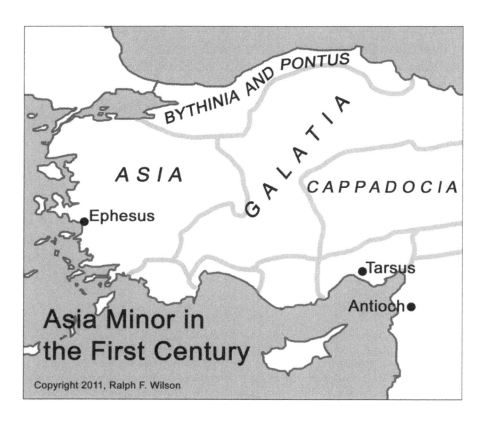

Paul obviously wrote Ephesians from prison (3:1; 4:1; 6:20), but prison where? We can't be sure, but likely in either Caesarea or Rome. Most who hold Pauline authorship date the Letter approximately 60 to 62 AD from Rome.

Ephesus in Paul's Day

The Letter seems to have been written to the Church at Ephesus (1:1), though it doesn't directly address problems in that church as do some other letters. It seems more like a tract than a personal letter, and was probably intended as a circular letter to be read in the house churches of Ephesus and western Asia Minor (the western portion of present-day Turkey).

Ephesus was founded by Ionian colonists about 1100 BC and over the next millennium ruled successively by the Persians, Greeks, Macedonians, and others. Rome ruled the city from 69 BC for the next 200 years. It prospered and became the provincial capital and leading city of the entire region. Estimates of its population in the first century begin at a quarter million inhabitants and go up from there.

Model of Temple of Artemis at Ephesus in Miniatürk Park, Istanbul, Turkey. Considered one of the 7 wonders of the ancient world.

It was famous for its temple to the goddess Artemis (Diana of Ephesus), a huge structure made of marble, 220 by 425 feet at its base, supported by beautiful pillars and rising to a height of 60 feet, considered one of the seven wonders of the ancient world. The city has been studied by archeologists since 1895 and the work continues. Some of the important buildings, present during Paul's ministry, include a huge theater on a hillside that could seat 24,000 people, mentioned in Acts 19:29ff. Others were the town hall (Prytaneion), the commercial market (Agora), baths and gymnasiums, a medical school, and a stadium 229 meters long and 30 meters wide built during Nero's reign (54-68 AD).

Besides the cult of Artemis, there is evidence of various mystery religions, the practice of magic (Acts 19:19), worship of Egyptian gods Sarapis and Isis, as well as devotion to large number of other deities: Agathe Tyche, Aphrodite, Apollo, Asclepius, Athena, the Cabiri, Concord, Cybele (the Mother Goddess), Demeter, Dionysus, Enedra, Hecate,

Hephaestus, Heracles, Hestia Boulaia, Kore, Nemesis, Pan, Pion (a mountain god), Pluto, Poseidon, Theos Hypsistos, Tyche Soteira, Zeus and several river deities.

A Jewish synagogue existed in Ephesus (Acts 19:8), though archeologists haven't discovered it yet. The Jewish community possessed citizenship, were exempted from military service, and granted freedom to practice their religion according to their traditions.[3]

Recipients of the Letter

But there's a real question whether Paul's Letter to the Ephesians was really intended for the Church at Ephesus. Let me explain. In verse 1, the phrase "in Ephesus" is missing in several early, reliable Greek manuscripts.[4] Probably the explanation is that the original letter was intended as a sort of circular letter for the Church at Ephesus as well as others in Asia Minor, to be read and then sent on. Since Ephesus was the best-known church in the area, the copy it made would be the source of most of the copies of the Letter made for others, probably inserting its own name in the first sentence. Indeed, the subjects in the Letter don't seem to be tied to the particular situation in Ephesus so much as in the churches in general. Nevertheless, we'll still refer to the Ephesian church as the primary recipient, even though there were probably other intended recipients, too.

Purpose, Themes, and Structure

Why was the Letter written? Since Paul's founding of the churches in the area around Ephesus, believers seem to have won many Gentiles to whom Paul's Letter is now directed. They were converts from a Hellenistic environment of mystery religions, magic, astrology, etc. They feared evil spirits and weren't sure about Christ's relationship to these forces. They also needed encouragement to adopt a lifestyle worthy of Christianity, free from drunkenness, sexual immorality, theft, and hatred. They also may have lacked respect for the Jewish heritage of their faith.

Paul uses a number of words in Ephesians that would have been familiar to his Gentile Christian readers from their former religions – head-body, fullness, mystery, age, ruler, etc. A century later this kind of terminology was used by full-blown Gnosticism. But Paul uses these words to demonstrate to his readers that Christ is far

---

[3] Information for this section came primarily from Clinton E. Arnold's articles: "Ephesians, Letter to the," DPL, pp. 238-249; and "Ephesus," DPL, pp. 249-253.

[4] "In Ephesus" is omitted in p[46] Aleph B 424[c] 1739 Basil, Origen, and apparently Marcion. The vast majority of the manuscripts include the phrase, but its absence in the early manuscripts provide strong external evidence for the omission of the place name as being original (O'Brien, p. 85, fn. 5).

above and superior to any hierarchy of gods and spiritual beings – that they are all lesser beings under Christ's feet. The language of Ephesians serves an apologetic function for the Church in a pluralistic society.[5]

The exact purpose of the Letter isn't fully clear, but it seems to fall along lines laid out by F.F. Bruce:

> "The Letter was written to encourage Gentile Christians to appreciate the dignity of their calling, with its implication not only for their heavenly origin and destiny, but also for their present conduct on earth, as those who were heirs of God, sealed with the Holy Spirit."[6]

Themes and Structure of the Letter

Paul develops several themes in this Letter:

1. The Greatness of God
2. The Exalted Christ
3. Salvation in the Present Dimension
4. The Status of Believers "in Christ"
5. The Unity of Jew and Gentile
6. The Struggle with Satanic Powers
7. The Ethical Obligations of Believers
8. The Apostle to the Gentiles
9. The Church

We'll be exploring each of these as we begin to look at the text.

The structure of Ephesians can be considered in halves. The first half, chapters 1 through 3, concern theological or doctrinal issues, while the second half, chapters 4 through 6, deal with ethical and practical outworkings of the Christian faith.

Reading Aloud

Ephesians is as inspiring as it is deep. It swells the soul in praise, encourages the mind in understanding, and warms the heart in giving thanks.

As you begin this study, immerse yourself in this short letter. Read the entire letter through several times – in different translations, if you can – to capture the big picture of what Paul is saying. As you read, let your spirit listen and soak up the wonderful truths.

---

[5] Edwin M. Yamauchi, "Gnosis, Gnosticism," DPL, pp. 350-354.
[6] Bruce, p. 245.

Reading aloud helps you hear with your ears what God is saying as these themes weave in and out, dancing with each other for sheer joy. You are about to expose yourself to one of the richest passages in all of Christian Scripture and literature.

Both Minds and Hearts

As you begin your study of Ephesians, I encourage you to give priority to prayerfulness rather than merely logical analysis. Paul's Letter to the Ephesians is designed to lift his readers from an earthly, worldly point of reference to a heavenly, spiritual one. While we'll analyze Paul's message and its implication, we must go beyond understanding to experience. Paul's prayer for us is "that you may know him better."

> "... That the eyes of your heart may be enlightened in order that you may know the hope to which he has called you, the riches of his glorious inheritance in the saints, and his incomparably great power for us who believe." (Ephesians 1:18-19a)

Prayer

Father, together we ask you that you might accomplish your purpose in our hearts and lives through this Letter to the Ephesians that your Spirit inspired Paul to write. Let us grow up in you to the full stature of Christ. In His holy name, we pray. Amen.

1. Spiritual Blessings in Christ (1:1-6)

As soon as Paul is finished with the preliminaries of opening the letter, he seems to break out in a psalm of praise – "Praise be to the God … who has blessed us…." Today's lesson overflows with all the blessings that we Christians are blessed with. God's wonderful generosity is on display.

Christ the Redeemer (*Cristo Redentor*, 1931), designed by Paul Landoviski (French-Polish monumental sculptor, 1875-1961) and built by engineer Heitor da Silva Costa, opens his arms in blessing (100 ft. statue on 20 ft. pedestal, on the 2,300-foot peak of Corcovado Mountain, overlooking Rio de Janeiro, Brazil).

Before we begin this passage, however, let me show you the big picture, since in just a moment we'll be focusing on the details. I want you to see both the "forest" *and* the "trees": In this passage and the next, which together make up the introduction to Ephesians, Paul tells us that we are:

In Christ

- Holy and blameless,
- Chosen,
- Adopted as sons and daughters of God, and
- Forgiven

and have been given:

- Knowledge of the mysteries of God
- A purpose to live for God's praise, and
- The Holy Spirit as a foretaste of future glory.

Now to the details!

Grace and Peace to the Saints (1:1-2)

Let's examine it verse-by-verse:

"Paul, an apostle of Christ Jesus by the will of God,
To the saints in Ephesus, the faithful in Christ Jesus:
Grace and peace to you from God our Father and the Lord Jesus Christ." (1:1-2)

I am immediately struck by three words in verse 1 – apostle, saints, and faithful.

"Apostle" (*apostolos*), "messenger, delegate, envoy," denotes a person sent with a specific commission or mission, from the verb *apostellō*, "to send."[1] Paul makes it clear from the start that he speaks with apostolic authority that comes directly from Jesus Christ. Moreover, he writes according to God's will. This is no casual communication, nor is it to be taken as just man's word, but as the words of Christ through Paul.

He addresses the letter to **"saints."** But saints aren't a bunch of people wearing halos; they are real, fallible people. "Saint" (*hagios*), when used of human beings, means "consecrated or dedicated to God, holy," that is, reserved for God and his service.[2] Saints aren't holy because we are perfect. We are holy because we are set apart and dedicated to God, because we belong to God exclusively. "You are not your own, you were bought at a price" (1 Corinthians 6:19-20).

The third word is **"faithful"** (*pistos*). The word means "trustworthy, faithful, dependable, inspiring of trust or faith."[3] Paul addresses the saints as faithful ones. Then he goes on to describe their location or relationship – "in Christ Jesus." We're more used to the phrase "Jesus Christ," but Paul sometimes uses the word order "Christ Jesus" (1:1 twice, 2:20; 3:1), emphasizing Jesus' title – "Messiah, Christ" along with his given name – "Jesus," which means "Yahweh saves."

Paul concludes his greeting with the words "Grace" – the characteristic Greek greeting – combined with "Peace" (Hebrew *shalom*), the characteristic Hebrew greeting.

Blessings in the Heavenly Realms (1:3)

One way to look at this letter is as a spontaneous outpouring of praise to God. It certainly begins that way. But now we find that the praise consists of an enumeration of God's great gifts to his children, his blessings.

"Blessed (*eulogētos*, "blessed, praised") be the God and Father of our Lord Jesus Christ, who has blessed (*eulogeō*) us in Christ with every spiritual blessing (*eulogia*) in the heavenly places...." (1:3, NRSV)

---

[1] *Apostellō*, BDAG 122.
[2] *Hagios*, BDAG 10-11.
[3] *Pistos*, BDAG 820-821.

It's pretty obvious that each of the three blessings in this verse are translations of closely related Greek words. The verb *eulogeō* means here "to bestow a favor, provide with benefits."[4] The noun *eulogia* is "the act or benefit of blessing."[5]

What we have here are the blessings come full circle, beginning with God ("who has blessed us … with every spiritual blessing") and finding their culmination in God ("blessed be the God and Father…."). God blesses us graciously, without any compulsion – just because he wants to. And we bless back, spontaneously, without any compulsion – because we are thankful and love God.

Notice two things about these blessings:

1. **They are "spiritual" (*pneumatikos*) blessings.** These aren't mere physical or natural blessings, but blessings of our spirit by God's Spirit. The blessing of knowledge, the blessing of love, the blessing of mercy, the blessing of salvation – the list goes on and on. He gives us *every* spiritual blessing. God is generous, not tight-fisted, in giving out his spiritual blessings.
2. **They are offered in the heavenly realm**, not the earthly realm. The Greek noun *epouranios*, can refer either to (1) the sky or heavens as an astronomical phenomenon, or, as here, to (2) pertaining to be associated with a locale for transcendent things and beings, "heavenly, in heaven."[6] We'll consider the implications of this further in Lesson 2.

In Christ

Ephesians introduces us to a phrase that we see throughout Paul's letters, but especially here – "in Christ." In the first 14 verses of this Letter, the phrase (or its equivalent) occurs 11 times:

1. "The faithful **in Christ Jesus**" (vs. 1)
2. "Every spiritual blessing **in Christ**" (vs. 3)
3. "Chose us **in him**" (vs. 4)
4. "Freely given us **in the One he loves**" (vs. 6)
5. "**In him** we have redemption" (vs. 7)
6. "Which he purposed **in Christ**" (vs. 9)

[4] *Eulogeō*, BDAG 408. The basic meaning is *eu*, "good" + *logia* "word, speaking."
[5] *Eulogia*, BDAG 408.
[6] *Epouranios*, BDAG 388.

7.   "To gather up all things **in him**" (vs. 10, NRSV)
8.   "**In him** we were also chosen" (vs. 11)
9.   "The first to hope **in Christ**" (vs. 12)
10. "Included **in Christ**" (vs. 13a)
11. "Marked **in him** with a seal" (vs. 13b)

Elsewhere in Ephesians it is found at 1:20; 2:6-7, 10, 13; 3:6, 11, 21; and 4:32. The common Greek preposition *en* seems to be used in one of two senses in the phrase "in Christ" as found in Ephesians:

> **Local (locative):** "In close association with."[7] Often the phrase seems to carry the idea of "incorporation into Christ."[8]
>
> **Instrumental**: "Marker introducing means or instrument, with, by means of."[9]

The preposition is used both ways in Ephesians, but I'm particularly intrigued by the local idea of incorporation into Christ, which I believe applies to most of the verses in our passage, especially in verse 11 where it talks about all creation being summed up in Christ as head. Likewise, in chapter 2 there are a remarkable number of compound verbs carrying the idea "together with," such as ""made alive with Christ" (2:5), "raised ... with Christ" (2:6a), "seated with him" (2:6b), etc. We are all "in Christ," part of him and he part of us. The primary idea of Ephesians is not Christ as the means by whom all these things come (though, of course, he *is* the means). Rather the primary idea is how we are joined with him in a spiritual sense. Our whole life is "in Christ." (See also Romans 5:12-19; 8:1; and 1 John 5:11-12.)

Q1. (Ephesians 1:3) What does it mean to you to be "in Christ" – incorporated into Christ? What are the implications of this for your life?
http://www.joyfulheart.com/forums/index.php?showtopic=527

---

[7] Frederick Danker notes this usage especially in Paul and John, "to designate a close personal relation in which the referent of the *en*-term is viewed as the controlling influence: under the control of, under the influence of, in close association with." *En*, BDAG 327-328, meanings 1 and 4.c, "Marker of a position defined as being in a location, "in, among," and by extension, "marker of close association within a limit, in." See also Albrecht Oepke, *en*, TDNT 2:537-543. "Being 'in Christ' expresses the operation of salvation in the field of force that Christ sets up" (Walter Grundmann, *chriō, ktl.*, TDNT 9:527-580).

[8] Bruce, 253, fn. 24.

[9] *En*, BDAG 328, 5b.

Predestination and Election (1:4-5)

Now, let's jump off the pier into deep water – predestination. This whole passage 1:3-14 is full of words that describe God purposing, planning, willing, and choosing from before the world's beginning.

I've heard people tell me that they don't believe in predestination. What they mean is that they don't believe what some people claim are the *results* of predestination, that exclude people from God's grace with no opportunity for redress. But if you believe the Bible, you believe in predestination, that is, you believe in God destining things to happen before they take place in our temporal world. Predestination is in the Bible in black and white.

Of course, none of us can pretend to really fathom predestination, much less understand it. So instead of trying to wrap your logical mind around predestination or rejecting it out of hand, just let these words of God's willing in this passage wash over you like a spring shower, reminding you that your God is greater than you and me and has planned much for us that is beyond our understanding! Look at this string of words:

1:1 – Paul, an apostle of Christ Jesus by the **will** (*thelēma*) of God."

1:4 – "For he **chose** (*eklegomai*) us in him before the creation of the world to be holy and blameless in his sight."

1:5 – "In love he **predestined** (*proorizō*) us to be adopted as his sons through Jesus Christ, in accordance with his **pleasure** (*eudokia*) and **will** (*thelēma*)...."

1:9 – "And he made known to us **the mystery of his will** (*thelēma*) according to **his good pleasure** (*eudokia*), which he **purposed** (*protithēmi*[10]) in Christ...."

1:11 – In him we were also **chosen** (*klēroō*[11]), having been **predestined** (*proorizō*) according to the **plan** (*prothesis*[12]) of him who works out everything in conformity with the **purpose** (*boulē*[13]) of his **will** (*thelēma*) ...."

The gist is that God has a plan that he is bringing to fruition and you and I are part of it. Now, let's consider verses 4 and 5 carefully:

[10] "Purposed" (NIV, KJV) or "set forth" (NRSV) used in verse 9 is the verb *protithēmi*, "set before." It can mean "set forth publicly" or to have something in mind beforehand, "plan, purpose, intend something," as in our passage (BDAG 889).

[11] "Chosen" (NIV) or "obtained an inheritance" (KJV, NRSV) in verse 11 is *klēroō*. The root idea of this word group is "lot," either a lot which is drawn in order to determine a decision or a portion of land assigned by lot. (BDAG 548-549. Werner Forester, *klēros, ktl.*, TDNT 3:758-769).

[12] "Plan" (NIV) or "purpose" (KJV, NRSV) in verse 11 is the noun *prothesis*, that which is planned in advance, "plan, purpose, resolve, will" (BDAG 869).

[13] "Purpose" (NIV) or "counsel" (KJV, NRSV) is the noun *boulē*, that which one decides, "resolution, decision" (BDAG 181-182).

"For he chose us in him before the creation of the world to be holy and blameless in his sight. In love he predestined us to be adopted as his sons through Jesus Christ, in accordance with his pleasure and will...." (1:4-5)

When Paul says, "he chose us in him before the creation of the world," he is speaking of choosing the Church, now largely Gentile as the Gospel has mushroomed and spread in the Mediterranean world. Let's examine some of these words related to planning and choosing:

"Chose" is the verb *eklegomai*, "to pick out, choose," from which we get our English word "election." Here it carries a reflexive idea, "select someone/something for oneself," to make a choice in accordance with significant preference.[14]

The next word, **"predestined"** focuses on the *time* of the choosing. "Predestined" (NIV), "predestinated" (KJV), and "destined" (NRSV) is the Greek verb *proorizō*, "decide upon beforehand, predetermine." The word is used only six times in the New Testament: Romans 8:29, 30; Acts 4:28; 1 Corinthians 2:7; and twice in our passage: 1:5 and 1:11.[15]

Another important word in our passage is **"will,"** used three times in verses 1, 5 and 11. The noun *thelēma*, "will" means "what one wishes to happen, what is willed."[16]

Enough Greek for a moment. It's pretty clear by his vocabulary that Paul is emphasizing that the Gentile Church is not some accident of history, but part of God's carefully conceived and executed plan, begun before the ages, before the world was created, which comes to focus in Jesus Christ our Lord.

Q2. (Ephesians 1:4-5) What is scary about predestination? What is comforting? Why does Paul bring up predestination? Why do you think he is praising God for it in the "hearing" of the Ephesians?
http://www.joyfulheart.com/forums/index.php?showtopic=528

Chosen for Holiness (1:4)

So far we've looked at the planning and choosing process. Now let's see what we were chosen to be and do.

---

[14] *Eklegomai*, BDAG 305.
[15] *Proorizō*, BDAG 873.
[16] *Thelēma*, BDAG 447.

"For he chose us in him before the creation of the world to be **holy and blameless** in his sight. In love he predestined us to be **adopted as his sons** through Jesus Christ...." (1:4-5)

What we chosen for is:

1. To be holy and blameless in his sight

   AND

2. To be adopted as sons

"Holy" (Greek *hagios*, the same word as "saints" in verse 1) means that we are consecrated to God, separated to him as his possession. God has claimed us and we belong to him.[17]

"Blameless" (Greek *amōmos*) means "without blemish" and was used of animals that were brought to the temple for sacrifice. These sacrificial animals given to God must be perfect – not lame or diseased.[18]

Notice the *sphere* of this holiness and blamelessness – "in his sight." Children misunderstand their relationship sometimes because they don't have enough experience to see themselves in perspective. A young teenager, for example, may feel gangly and self-conscious with physical changes that are taking place rapidly. I'm ugly, he might think or she might imagine. But in the parent's eyes, the youngster may be quite on track in development appropriate to his or her age.

God has forgiven our sins through Jesus Christ. Now he sees us as "holy" – completely, wholly his – and "blameless" – one who can stand before his throne with a slate wiped clean of any sin or imperfection.

Q3. (Ephesians 1:4) What does it mean to be "holy"? In what sense can you stand "blameless" before God?

http://www.joyfulheart.com/forums/index.php?showtopic=529

---

[17] *Hagios*, BDAG 10-11.
[18] *Amōmos*, BDAG 56.

Chosen to Be Adopted (1:5-6)

Now Paul introduces another concept that has been in the mind of God from before the beginning – adoption (Greek *hiothesia*).

> "In love he predestined us to be **adopted as his sons** through Jesus Christ, in accordance with his pleasure and will – to the praise of his glorious grace, which he has freely given us in the One he loves." (1:5-6)

In Paul's day, one could move from the lowest class to the highest by means of adoption. A beloved slave could be freed (manumitted) and then adopted by a Roman citizen. Upon adoption, the slave became a son, an heir, and a citizen. An adopted son now had the same rights and privileges as a naturally-born son.[19]

(Incidentally, Paul's term "adoption as sons" includes women Christians also, but to be culturally accurate with the analogy, the position and privileges of sons were much greater than those of daughters in the Mediterranean world. In the Kingdom of God women and men inherit fully and equally. Hallelujah!)

You can't entirely blame parents for who their children become. Kids have a way of sometimes being very different from their biological parents. But we are blessed by being adopted into God's family because God, knowing fully who we are (including our weaknesses, foibles, and sins) wanted us in particular and so adopted us. We aren't in God's family by happenstance of birth (to continue with the adoption analogy), but by God's choice. God loves you!

Q4. (Ephesians 1:5-6) Why is adoption a particularly apt illustration of God's relationship with us? Why is the concept of adoption encouraging to us?
http://www.joyfulheart.com/forums/index.php?showtopic=530

Prayer

Our Father, we thank you so much for the love of God that you have included us in Jesus Christ. Give us an experience of the richness of the family of God into which we have been adopted. In Jesus' name, we pray. Amen.

Key Verses

> "Praise be to the God and Father of our Lord Jesus Christ, who has blessed us in the heavenly realms with every spiritual blessing in Christ." (Ephesians 1:3)

---

[19] *Hiothesia*, BDAG 1024.

"For he chose us in him before the creation of the world to be holy and blameless in his sight." (Ephesians 1:4)

2. God's Plan of Redemption (1:7-14)

In the first part of Paul's introductory section we considered some of God's blessings. He has blessed us in viewing us as holy and blameless. He has blessed us with adoption and the full inheritance of his own sons. He has blessed us by predestining us to live for his glory. And now another "spiritual blessing in heavenly places" – redemption.

Redemption through His Blood (1:7-8)

> "In him we have redemption through his blood, the forgiveness of sins, in accordance with the riches of God's grace that he lavished on us with all wisdom and understanding." (1:7-8)

Our culture doesn't think of redemption, since we haven't had legal slavery for 150 years. But in Paul's day slavery was very much the norm among the poor in the cities of the Mediterranean. Many of the early Christians were slaves (6:5-8). To them, redemption meant freedom. "Redemption" (*apolutrōsis*) originally referred to "buying back" a slave or captive, that is "making free" by payment of a ransom. Here it means release from a captive condition, "release, redemption," figuratively of the release from sin that comes though Christ.[1]

Thomas Eakins (American painter, 1844-1916), "The Crucifixion" (1880), Oil on canvas, 96 x 54 inches, Philadelphia Museum of Art.

The payment price to buy us back from our slavery to sin was "his blood." Some Christians seem offended by this, that Christ's blood should be the ransom price. Blood sacrifice harkens back to some primitive religion, they mutter. Some hymnals, in fact, have expurgated nearly every hymn that mentions the blood of Christ as being the atoning sacrifice for our sins.

However, this figure is based squarely on the Old Testament sacrificial system of a lamb or other animal being slain for the sins of the people. Animal sacrifice for atonement of sin was God's way of teaching principles of holiness and sin, forgiveness

[1] *Apolutrōsis*, BDAG 117.

and grace to the early Israelites. In the New Testament, the concept is mentioned numerous times.[2]

If you remove Christ's blood from Christianity, his death becomes a mere symbol, sin becomes only human frailty, the results of sin an earthly tragedy, and love and grace are present without any righteousness or justice.

I believe we must take Paul quite seriously when he says rather plainly, "In him we have redemption through his blood, the forgiveness of sins" (1:7). A price has been paid to set us free from the bondage of sin,[3] and that price is Christ's death on the cross. Mel Gibson's "The Passion of the Christ" (Newmarket Films, 2004) has been criticized for its gratuitous violence. But he got the important parts right. The issue that was tearing Jesus apart in the Garden of Gethsemane as the film begins is the horror of bearing in his human flesh the sins of all mankind. "You're not strong enough," says Satan, in the film. But on the cross, Jesus calls out in triumph, "It is accomplished!" His death bought our freedom.

Q1. (Ephesians 1:7) In what sense have you been "redeemed" from slavery? What do you think your life up to now would have been like, if you hadn't been redeemed? What would your future be like without redemption, do you think?
http://www.joyfulheart.com/forums/index.php?showtopic=497

Grace Lavished on Us (1:8)

The great prize was won, however, at a staggering cost. What an immense act of grace and courage and mercy! Paul completes his sentence with a paean of praise:

> "In him we have redemption through his blood, the forgiveness of sins, in accordance with the riches of God's grace that he lavished on us with all wisdom and understanding." (1:7-8)

What does it mean "in accordance with the riches of God's grace"? "Grace" is the noun *charis*, "a beneficent disposition toward someone, favor, grace, gracious care or

---

[2] See Matthew 20:28; 26:28 || Mark 14:24; Acts 20:28b; Hebrews 9:14, 22; 1 Peter 1:18-19; 1 John 2:2; Revelation 5:9. For more on this see my book, *Lamb of God* (JesusWalk Publications, 2011). www.jesuswalk.com/ebooks/lamb.htm

[3] "Forgiveness" is the noun *aphesis*, "the act of freeing and liberating from something that confines, release from captivity." Here it refers to "the act of freeing from an obligation, guilt, or punishment, pardon, cancellation" (BDAG 155).

help, goodwill."[4] Grace, simply, is favor towards someone. Not an earned response from a superior, but favor bestowed simply because it pleases the Giver.

Paul is saying that our redemption and forgiveness are "in accordance with" (*kata*[5]), or "to the extent of" the wealth, riches, or abundance (*ploutos*[6]) of God's favor. In other words, our redemption is not barely enough, but plenteous. Our forgiveness is not scarcely, but abundantly given.

God has not just gone through the motions, just enough to get by, but his grace has been "lavished upon us." "Lavished" (NIV, NRSV) and "abounded" (KJV) is the verb *perisseuō*, "to be in abundance, abound."[7] The picture we are given is of overflowing love, surpassing grace, a cherishing by God that is much more than enough for us – and certainly undeserved! Meditate on that! *That*, dear friends, is what Paul is saying to us in this verse.

Uniting All Things in Christ (1:9-10)

Note carefully the next verses which serve as a theme for the entire book of Ephesians:

> "And he made known to us the mystery of his will according to his good pleasure, which he purposed in Christ, to be put into effect when the times will have reached their fulfillment – to bring all things in heaven and on earth together under one head, even Christ." (1:9-10)

Paul speaks of a "mystery" (Greek *mustērion*), used in the sense of a "revelation of what was previously hidden but has now been disclosed by God."[8] What is this mystery? In both Ephesians and Colossians the mystery refers to the ultimate fulfillment in the end times[9] of God's plan of salvation in Christ. Sometimes one aspect of this is the focus: Gentiles along with Jews are being saved. But here the mystery is universal in scope.

---

[4] *Charis*, BDAG 1079-1081.

[5] *Kata* here is a "marker of norm of similarity or homogeneity, according to, in accordance with, in conformity with, according to" (BDAG 511-513).

[6] *Ploutos*, BDAG 832.

[7] Here *perisseuō* has the causative idea, "to cause something to exist in abundance, cause to abound" (BDAG 805).

[8] O'Brien 109.

[9] "Fulfillment" (NIV) and "fullness" (KJV, NRSV) is the noun *plērōma*, "fullness," here refers to "the state of being full," "fullness of time" (also in Galatians 4:4) (BDAG 829-830). "Times" is the noun *kairos*, "a period of time" (BDAG 497-498).

The key idea contained in the Greek word *anakephalaioō* is "to sum up," variously translated "to bring ... together under one head" (NIV), "gather together in one" (KJV), and "to gather up all things" (NRSV). It is a rare word, compounded from *ana-* "again" + *kephalaioomai* "bring to a head" (from *kephalē*, "head"). It carries the ideas of "to gather up, to sum up, recapitulate," and is found in the New Testament elsewhere only at Romans 13:9.[10]

The point is that in Christ – not in the church nor in Judaism – will everything be summed up. Not only the believers of God's people but "all things in heaven and on earth." Christ is to be the all and in all, the sum of the parts.

Q2. (Ephesians 1:9-10) What is the significance that all things will be brought under one head – Christ himself? How does this relate to the Creator? What does it say about unity? *Extra Credit:* **How does this verse relate to 1 Corinthians 15:24-28?**
http://www.joyfulheart.com/forums/index.php?showtopic=499

Predestined for Praise (1:11-12)

> "In him we were also chosen, having been predestined according to the plan of him who works out everything in conformity with the purpose of his will, in order that we, who were the first to hope in Christ, might be for the praise of his glory." (1:11-12)

In chapter one of this study we considered the words "predestined," "plan," "purpose," and "will." Here notice the *purpose* of this predestination: "that we ... might be for the praise of his glory." Our purpose is praise. "Praise" is the noun *epainos*, "the act of expressing admiration or approval, praise, approval, recognition."[11]

Have you ever wondered why you are here? Why you were spared in some dangerous accident? Why you are still living, even though you might have been an invalid? We don't know everything God is doing, but we do know this: He has destined us to live for his praise. When people look at you, Jesus intends that they see God. "In the same way, let your light shine before men, that they may see your good deeds and praise your Father in heaven" (Matthew 5:16)

God has placed you as a light. God has made you a mirror – to reflect his glory and help people see a glimmer of his greatness living in human flesh. You have an important

---

[10] O'Brien 112-113; Bruce 261 fn. 71; Heinrich Schlier, *kephalē*, TDNT 3:673-682; BDAG 55-56.

[11] *Epainos*, BDAG 357. Purpose here is expressed by the preposition *eis*, 4. "a marker of goals involving affective/abstract/suitability aspects, into, to" (BDAG 288-291).

purpose on this earth, no matter how unimportant you may feel. You have been placed here to bring praise to God!

Q3. (Ephesians 1:11-12) According to verses 11 and 12, what is God's purpose for our lives? What do we need to do to fulfill this purpose? How does this purpose relate to Matthew 5:13-16?
http://www.joyfulheart.com/forums/index.php?showtopic=500

Sealed by the Spirit as a Guarantee (1:13-14)

Do you feel like Paul is talking about someone else? He is not. He is speaking of *you*.

"And *you also* were included in Christ when you heard the word of truth, the gospel of your salvation. Having believed, you were marked in him with a seal, the promised Holy Spirit, who is a deposit guaranteeing our inheritance until the redemption of those who are God's possession – to the praise of his glory." (1:13-14)

So that you might be sure that you are included, he has put his mark on you – the Holy Spirit. The phrase "marked with a seal" (NIV, NRSV) or "sealed" (KJV) is the verb *sphragizō*, "to mark with a seal as a means of identification, mark, seal."[12] You've probably played with sealing wax and a bronze seal or a seal on a ring, so you understand the idea. We see the word again later in the letter: "And do not grieve the Holy Spirit of God, with whom you were sealed for the day of redemption" (4:30). The seal is a mark of identification and of protection against tampering, until the day it is intended to be opened, "the day of redemption,"[13] the day of Christ's return and the rapture of the church.

Paul has a two-fold analogy for the Holy Spirit: (1) a seal and (2) a deposit. The phrase "deposit guaranteeing" (NIV), "earnest" (KJV), and "pledge" (NRSV) is the noun *arrabōn*, a legal and commercial technical term meaning payment of a part of a purchase price in advance, "first installment, deposit, down payment, pledge," which secures a legal claim to the article in question, or makes a contract valid.[14]

The Holy Spirit has a way of bringing a bit of heaven into our lives here on earth. Through the Holy Spirit, God can speak to us and we to God. In the Holy Spirit the incredible power of the Kingdom of God can work in and through us. The Holy Spirit

---

[12] *Sphragizō*, BDAG 980.
[13] "Redemption" is *apolutrōsis*, as in 1:7 above.
[14] *Arrabōn*, BDAG 134.

was obviously someone whom the Ephesian Christians were aware of in their lives. Paul says to them: This Holy Spirit that now lets you glimpse God and heaven is like a deposit on the full amount, literally "a foretaste of glory divine."[15]

You as God's Possession (1:14)

Look at these verses again in terms of being God's possession:

"Having believed, you were marked in him with a seal, the promised Holy Spirit, who is a deposit guaranteeing our inheritance until the redemption of those who are *God's possession* – to the praise of his glory." (1:13-14)

Here is another reminder, Christian friend, that you are "God's possession" (NIV), "purchased possession" (KJV), and "God's own people" (NRSV). The Greek noun is *peripoiēsis*, "that which is acquired, "possessing, possession, property."[16] "You are not your own, you were bought at a price" (1 Corinthians 6:19-20). This is another reference to the redemption of slaves.

Q4. (1:13-14) These verses contain two analogies: (1) seal and (2) down payment, with the balance to be paid in a lump sum at the end of the term. When does the "end of the term" occur? How do these analogies help explain how the Holy Spirit functions in our lives?
http://www.joyfulheart.com/forums/index.php?showtopic=501

Full Citizens

Some people think that Ephesians was written to help Gentile Christians get over their inferiority complex and understand that they are every bit as much God's people as the Jewish people – and I think I agree. As individuals, too, we can have an inferiority complex – a feeling that we aren't good enough. That if only God knew what we were really like he wouldn't love us. Our passage is designed to help *you* get over *your* inferiority complex.

Let the words of this passage remind you that this is no illusion, but a glorious fact – called, chosen, forgiven, redeemed, adopted, sealed with the Holy Spirit. God's great blessings are for us who do not deserve them. That is what grace is about. That is what the Gospel is about. And that is why this grace and gospel are so amazing and

[15] The phrase is from the hymn "Blessed Assurance" (1873) by Fanny Crosby.
[16] *Peripoiēsis*, BDAG 804.

wonderful. Three centuries ago a former slave trader, John Newton, penned these beloved words:

> "Amazing grace,
> How sweet the sound that saved a wretch like me.
> I once was lost, but now I'm found.
> Was blind, but now I see."

Prayer

Lord, thank you for your amazing grace and love. Thank you for including us in your purpose and plan. Help me to bring praise and glory to you. In Jesus' name, I pray. Amen.

Key Verses

"In him we have redemption through his blood, the forgiveness of sins, in accordance with the riches of God's grace that he lavished on us with all wisdom and understanding." (Ephesians 1:7-8)

"Having believed, you were marked in him with a seal, the promised Holy Spirit, who is a deposit guaranteeing our inheritance until the redemption of those who are God's possession – to the praise of his glory." (Ephesians 1:13-14)

3. The Greatness of Our Christian Inheritance (1:15-23)

I've found that I need my wife to see things that I don't, to understand people's emotions better. I can be so dull sometimes, so blind. Then she'll say something about watching their body language and listening to their heart, and I'll say, "Oh."

We can be just as dull when it comes to Christianity. The limits of our own personal participation in how God works may be small. People in our local fellowship may be limited in faith or love or experience. And so our understanding of the gospel can be constrained, tiny, narrow.

A bowl of fruit, a symbol of the abundance of the Christian inheritance in heaven, decorates a third century Christian burial place (Catacomb of St. Sebastian Rome, columbarium, fresco).

The passage we're studying is a definite vision-expander. Paul helped pioneer the church at Ephesus, but now it's been years since he's seen them. Many new people have joined the congregation, but he prays for them. He hears of the astounding faith and love of people in this church (1:15) and rejoices. "I have not stopped giving thanks for you, remembering you in my prayers" (1:16). He prays and rejoices, and then asks for a special revelation to come to them. He prays that God will take off their blinders and expand their minds so that they can understand the hugeness of the faith, "so that you may know him better" (1:17b).

A Great Vision (1:17-19a)

"I keep asking that the God of our Lord Jesus Christ, the glorious Father, may give you the Spirit of wisdom and revelation, so that you may know him better. I pray also that the eyes of your heart may be enlightened in order that you may know the hope to which he has called you, the riches of his glorious inheritance in the saints, and his incomparably great power for us who believe." (Ephesians 1:17-19a)

The content of Paul's prayer for their enlightenment is three-fold. As I read his prayer, I see a big, three-dimensional Valentine with eyes (and maybe eyelashes, I don't know). The big eyes on this red heart are closed. Not closed tightly, but closed. "I pray," Paul says, "that the eyes of your heart may be enlightened…" (1:18a). One eye begins to open a little, and then another. The big Valentine winces a bit as it gets adjusted to the light that is now starting to come in through squinted eyes. Wow, I can see things out there I didn't even know existed. The other eye opens as Paul prays for a specific aspect of revelation. The heart with closed eyes has now become an excited heart, beating wildly with joy and anticipation as it begins to see new things, understand new truths. "I pray that the eyes of your heart may be enlightened" (1:18a).

Hope to Which He Has Called You (1:18b)

First, he prays that they "may know the hope to which he has called you." Hope in this verse (Greek *elpis*) is not some wishy-washy "hope so" desire, but a firm expectation – "the looking forward to something with some reason for confidence respecting fulfillment, hope, expectation."[1] This is eager watchfulness. We can become bored, lazy, hopeless, listless. Jesus Christ is the "hope of glory" for us (Colossians 1:27b). Christ's return is our "blessed hope" (Titus 2:13). Jesus provides the expectation that he will work through our prayers and our hands. Jesus Christ provides the hope that motivates us that the future with him will be better.

We have been called to a future and a hope (Jeremiah 29:11). It is our calling to look forward, to anticipate, even to hasten Christ's coming in power and in glory (2 Peter 3:12). Paul prays for our hope to expand and embrace a big future, rather than shrivel in pain, bitterness, and discouragement or die in a parched desert of spiritual starvation. To a grand view of our future in Jesus Christ we have been called, brothers and sisters. Our hope – when we catch this view – is truly glorious!

Q1. (Ephesians 1:18b) What do we Christians have to look forward to? How should this hope be a major motivation in our present-day lives? How should this hope affect our decisions and our lifestyle? How does our great hope differ from the hope of the average non-believer?
http://www.joyfulheart.com/forums/index.php?showtopic=502

His Glorious Inheritance in the Saints (1:18c)

Second, Paul wants us to know "the riches of his glorious inheritance[2] in the saints." What is an inheritance? It consists of the carefully accumulated possessions of another,

---

[1] *Elpis*, BDAG 319-320.

[2] "Inheritance" is *klēronomia*, the common word for "inheritance," then "possession, property." Here it is used of our possession of "transcendent salvation," as the inheritance of God's children (BDAG 547-548).

set aside and preserved to pass on to one's heirs. Ours is a "glorious inheritance," Paul says – an inheritance which is attended by glory, which consists of glory in his presence, and which makes us rich beyond all comparison.

We are to comprehend the degree of the riches of his inheritance. Greek *ploutos* means "wealth, abundance, plentiful supply."[3] It is not meager but abundant, overflowing, beyond counting.

We live lives of struggle and hurt, of love and of reaching out, but we fall so short. Paul prays that we will be able to comprehend that which we have ahead of us as a reward above all measure – a precious redemption purchased at great cost by our Brother, Jesus Christ. Someone described GRACE as an acronym – "God's Riches At Christ's Expense." An inheritance. But more than that, it is an inheritance "in the saints." Ours is not a solo award, but one we will share forever and ever with all God's people, living and dead. Oh, don't worry, there's plenty for all. But it is shared with the family.

Sometimes we are tempted to isolate ourselves from others. We've suffered too much rejection, we have some "history" that makes us love-shy, and so we practice our own form of hermit-Christianity. But our inheritance is "in the saints," as part of a corporate body.

Q2. (Ephesians 1:18c) If you knew that in a few years you would inherit $10 million, would it affect your life now? How should our expectation of an inheritance in God's presence temper our present-day concerns? Since this inheritance will be shared with "the saints" – our Christian family – how should that affect our fellowship with them?
http://www.joyfulheart.com/forums/index.php?showtopic=503

His Incomparably Great Power (1:18d)

First, hope. Second, inheritance. Third, Paul prays that we might know "his incomparably great power for (*eis*) us who believe." The Greek preposition *eis* often carries a sense of motion, "into, in, toward, to" and sometimes as a marker of goals.[4] The use here could carry the idea of power directed (1) "into us," "toward us," or (2) "for our benefit." While it's difficult to say which it is precisely, the idea is still wonderful!

---

[3] *Ploutos*, BDAG 832.
[4] *Eis*, BDAG 288-291.

In this case, God's immeasurable power is into and unto us believers. It is "incomparably great" – a pair of Greek words. *Hyperballō* means "to attain a degree that extraordinarily exceeds a point on a scale of extent, go beyond, surpass, outdo."[5] The second word is *megethos*, "greatness, a quality of exceeding a standard of excellence."[6] Paul heaps one word upon another to impress upon us the extreme, humongous, immeasurable nature of the power. God's full horsepower at our disposal, working in us who believe.

What is this power (Greek *dynamis*), this "might, strength, force, capability"?[7] Jesus said,

> "I tell you the truth: It is good for you that I am going away. Unless I go away, the Counselor will not come to you, but if I go, I will send him to you." (John 14:6-7)

He promised, "You shall receive power when the Holy Spirit comes upon you" (Acts 1:8a). And because this Counselor, the Holy Spirit, now lives inside of us, with us at the very deepest level, we will do greater things than even Jesus' miracles (John 14:12).

You see, the very same power that empowered Jesus' ministry on earth dwells in us. The very same power that called Lazarus to come out of the tomb lives in you in the presence of the Third Person of the Trinity. The power in the hands that touched blind eyes and made them see, that broke bread and fishes and fed 5,000 is in you.

But I don't see anything of the kind, you say. I feel powerless. Perhaps, but the scripture says that you are filled with incomparably great power toward us who believe, "like (Greek *kata*, "in accordance with, just as, similar to"[8]) as his mighty strength which he (God) exerted in Christ when he raised him from the dead."

I don't see it, you contend. Exactly. Laying hold of this power today is a function of our faith. It is a function of seeing the truth in our hearts and then acting upon it. That is why Paul is praying diligently that the eyeballs of your heart may be opened, that your blindness be cured, that your faith be broadened. And mine too.

In the past we have lived far below our hope, our inheritance, and our power. But we need live there no longer. God is opening our eyes and stirring up our faith.

> "'No eye has seen, no ear has heard, no mind has conceived what God has prepared for those who love him' – *but God has revealed it to us by his Spirit*." (1 Corinthians 2:9-10)

---

[5] *Hyperballō*, BDAG 1032.
[6] *Megethos*, BDAG 624-625.
[7] *Dynamis*, BDAG 262-263.
[8] *Kata*, BDAG 511-513, 5b.

Q3. (Ephesians 1:18d) Why are we powerless sometimes? Is it an inadequacy with the source or with our faith? Why do some congregations and movements produce disciples with miracle-believing faith and others produce disciples with wimpy faith? How can this be changed?

http://www.joyfulheart.com/forums/index.php?showtopic=504

A Great Christ (1:19b-23)

> "That power is like the working of his mighty strength, which he exerted in Christ when he raised him from the dead and seated him at his right hand in the heavenly realms, far above all rule and authority, power and dominion, and every title that can be given, not only in the present age but also in the one to come. And God placed all things under his feet and appointed him to be head over everything for the church, which is his body, the fullness of him who fills everything in every way." (Ephesians 1:19b-23)

Paul's prayer for the Ephesian Christians – and for us – runs into praise for his Jesus. His Christ is not but a pleasant memory, a hallowed tradition, or a sacred icon. His Christ is a living Victor.

First, God raised him from the dead. God broke the power of death which held Christ, and set him free forever, the first-fruits of the resurrection. Jesus' resurrection, as we'll see in the next chapter of our study, prefigures our own.

Second, Paul's Christ has been seated at God's right hand, the place of power and authority, of co-regency with God the Father.

Third, this "realm" (NIV) of the "heavenlies" (KJV) is a place of spiritual authority over every created being – animal, vegetable, mineral, demon or angel, saint or sinner, over every other pretentious name or title or position of honor in this world or the next. You may be impressed by your boss's title and position. Christ is far over him. The glamour and glitter of this world catches our eyes and sometimes our hearts. Christ is exalted over all of this. All this will come and go and turn to dust and ashes, but Christ will remain.

We see the term "heavenly places, realms" (Greek *epoura-nios*)[9] again in vs. 20b, which we first saw in 1:3, and which appear again in 2:6 and 6:12. It refers to the unseen spiritual realm in which dwell God, angels, and various members of a kind of evil demonic hierarchy: "rule, authority, power, and dominion" (vs. 21). The secular world, and especially the scientific community, used to deny the existence of the spiritual realm. But then came Star Wars which popularized "the dark side of the Force." There has been a string of TV shows touching on spiritual phenomena – angels, mediums, necromancers, etc. – which have helped our society to become aware of the reality of the spirit world, no matter how far these shows may have departed from a Scriptural understanding. The heavenly realm is a place of struggle with evil (6:12) which can be overcome day by day only through God's spiritual "armor" and power.

Detail of stele of pink sandstone commemorating the Victory of Naram-suen/Naramsin "Grandson of Sargon" over the "Lullubi people" (2230 B.C), Lourve, Paris. See how the necks of the enemies are "under his feet."

Fourth, God has placed all things under Christ's feet. This is a military expression in which the victor in battle demonstrates his superiority over his defeated foes. They are not only under his feet in spiritual authority, but he has conquered them and become head over them. You may not see it in your corner of the world yet, but it has been done. The decisive battle was fought and won at Calvary and the Empty Tomb. The rest is just a mop-up operation to secure the victory to every realm and place on this earth. In a sense, you are part of the Occupation Force for Jesus where you live, work, study, and play, and part of an Expeditionary Force to extend his victory to its logical conclusion among every tribe, people group, and nation on the face of the earth.

---

[9] *Epouranios*, "pertaining to being associated with a locale for transcendent things and beings, heavenly, in heaven" (BDAG 388).

Christ as Head (1:22)

In Ephesians we see the idea of "head" or "head and body" four times.

1:10 – "… When the times will have reached their fulfillment – to **bring** all things in heaven and on earth **together under one head** (*anakephalaioō*), even Christ."

1:22-23 – "And God placed all things under his feet and appointed him to be **head** over everything for the church, which is his **body**…."

4:15-16 – "… We will in all things grow up into him who is the **Head**, that is, Christ. From him the whole **body** … grows and builds itself up in love, as each part does its work."

5:23 – "For the husband is the **head** of the wife as Christ is the **head** of the church, his **body**, of which he is the Savior."

The Greek noun for "head" is *kephalē*. It means first the physical head, and then extends to a figurative use as "being of high status, head." With living beings, *kephalē* refers to superior rank.[10] *Kephalē* is a key concept in Ephesians that we'll consider in greater detail later.

Q4. (Ephesians 1:20-22) Why do we so often take a "pass" when it comes to spiritual warfare? Why is Christ's exaltation, demonstration of complete victory, and superior rank over all spiritual powers important enough for Paul to mention it to his readers? Why do we tend to feel powerless in the face of spiritual enemies? What was Paul assuring the Ephesians of? What does this encourage us to do?
http://www.joyfulheart.com/forums/index.php?showtopic=505

A Great Church (1:22-23)

"And God placed all things under his feet and appointed him to be head over everything *for the church,* which is his body, the fullness of him who fills everything in every way." (Ephesians 1:22-23)

This passage concludes with a marvelous vision of the Church. The word "church" used in vs. 23 is Greek *ekklēsia*, from *ek,* "out" + *kaleō*, "to call," with the root idea of "the called-out ones." Classical Greek used *ekklēsia* to refer to a "regularly summoned legislative body, assembly."[11] In the Septuagint (a Greek translation of the Old

---

[10] *Kephalē*, BDAG 541-542.
[11] *Eklēssia*, BDAG 303-304.

Testament) it means "the Jewish congregation." This is not a "mystical church" idea so much as an assembled group of people. The book of Ephesians has a very high view of the local congregation, much higher than both the world and church members who act as if the church were merely a human institution.

"Pooh! The church," I hear people say. "That sorry institution? Pooh!" Yes, *your* church, maybe. But notice three things about *Christ's* church:

First, the church is the recipient of Christ's conquering and headship over all things. It is *"for* the church."[12] Christ values the church extremely highly, since his work is to directly benefit the church.

Second, the church is his Body. He is the head, we are the body, the hands and fingers, the voices and feet. We are Christ's music and spokesmen, his messengers and workers, his lovers-of-humanity and his clear eyes of acceptance and forgiveness and love. We are his representatives. Don't tell me the church is obsolete! We have a great calling as Christ's body, and we've just begun to learn how to be little christs ("Christians") in his world.

Third and last, we, the church, are the fullness (*plērōma*)[13] of Christ, who fills and fulfills everything. We are to be the full expression of Christ. We are to be so filled with Christ that our content becomes Him, that our love becomes blended with His love, that our laughter echoes his own joy, that our sacrifice mirrors his. We are to be the fullness of Christ. Indeed, we are "complete in Him" (*plērōma*, KJV, Colossians 2:10).

No wonder Paul prayed for the Ephesians, prayed that their eyes might be opened. His prayer extends to our eyes also.

Q5. (Ephesians 1:22-23) When we neglect to be an active part of a local congregation, what particular blessings do we miss out on according to Paul in this verse? How do we, by our absence, withhold this blessing from others?

http://www.joyfulheart.com/forums/index.php?showtopic=506

---

[12] Dative of object.

[13] *Plērōma*, can refer to "that which fills" as well as "that which is full of something," which is the idea in our verse. A century or two later, *plērōma* was a Gnostic technical term. In Paul's day the term was used in the mystery religions, but not with the full Gnostic meaning. It is used four times in Ephesians (1:10, 23; 3:19; 4:13) (BDAG 829-830).

Prayer

Lord Jesus, open our eyes, too! Help us to be deeply dissatisfied with our own meager level of Christian understanding and practice. Help us to seek you, yearn for you, long to see and experience and enter into more. Help us to see and follow in the fresh footprints of the Victorious Christ as he walks in our world. Lord, open our eyes and hearts to you. Amen.

Key Verses

"And God placed all things under his feet and appointed him to be head over everything for the church, which is his body, the fullness of him who fills everything in every way." (Ephesians 1:22-23)

4. From Deadness to Coming Alive in Christ (2:1-7)

Our passage runs in the face of our culture. A generation or two ago, the culture understood the concept of sin. Today, a large portion of our culture rejects absolute truth, and consequently any concept of sin – at least at an intellectual level. Of course, this don't stop the powerful combination of the conscience and the Holy Spirit to convict the person of sin, of righteousness, and of judgment (John 16:8-11). Consequently, many nonbelievers have a sense of guilt, but no intellectual framework in which to understand it and thus no way to relieve that guilt of sin without explaining it away – which is ultimately unsatisfactory.

The temptation in the garden is not the story of man vs. woman, but the story of Satan blinding humankind with his enticements. Detail of William Blake (1757-1827), "Eve tempted by the serpent" (1799-1800), gum and gold on copper, Victoria and Albert Museum, London.

Dead in Transgressions and Sin (2:1)

But it is vital that we Christians understand what is going on. Paul writes:

> "¹As for you, you were dead in your transgressions and sins, ²in which you used to live when you followed the ways of this world and of the ruler of the kingdom of the air, the spirit who is now at work in those who are disobedient. ³All of us also lived among them at one time, gratifying the cravings of our sinful nature and following its desires and thoughts. Like the rest, we were by nature objects of wrath. (2:1-3)

Paul says that people without Christ are spiritually "dead" – dead in transgressions and sins. Our culture doesn't even like to use the word sin. Transgression? Transgression of what?

The word "transgressions" (NIV) or "trespasses" (NRSV, KJV) is the Greek noun *paraptōma*, "a violation of moral standards, offense, wrongdoing, sin."[1] The word, of course, assumes a divine law. "Sins" is the Greek *harmatia*, the most commonly used word for sin in the New Testament, literally "a missing of the mark." But the word is not

---

[1] *Paraptōma*, BDAG 770.

used in the New Testament of trivial, involuntary mistakes, but of serious offences against God, "a departure from either human or divine standards of uprightness."[2]

Our culture doesn't really believe in any absolute truth, so the idea of transgression or trespass of divine law is foreign to us. But whether or not we understand or believe it, our transgressions and sins against God's holy law have made us dead to God. Spiritually dead. And whether our age understands deadness to God, they *do* understand and experience emptiness. No wonder our culture is so interested in spirituality and hungry for spiritual fulfillment. Yes, our culture is vulnerable to the promises of the New Age movement – but it is also potentially open to the power of a vibrant Christian faith!

Q1. (Ephesians 2:1-3) In what sense are our non-believing friends, neighbors, and relatives "dead"? What's the difference between us and them? If we really believed that they were "dead" and subject to God's "wrath," what would we do?
http://www.joyfulheart.com/forums/index.php?showtopic=507

Following Satan (2:2-3)

"[... Transgressions and sins] in which you used to live when you followed the ways of this world and of the ruler of the kingdom of the air, the spirit who is now at work in those who are disobedient. All of us also lived among them at one time, gratifying the cravings of our sinful nature and following its desires and thoughts. Like the rest, we were by nature objects of wrath." (2:2-3)

"The power of the air" (vs. 2) is an interesting expression. "Power" (KJV, RSV) is Greek *exousia*, "authority," "the power exercised by rulers or others in high position by virtue of their office," then "the sphere in which the power is exercised, domain"[3] "Air" is a transliteration of Greek *aēr*. Great airy tomes have been written about what this word signifies. The Greeks saw heaven as the abode of the gods, earth the abode of humans, and the air as the abode of the demons.[4] I think this is Paul's reference: to Satan as the prince of demons. Period. Paul didn't have to adopt Greek cosmology to employ it in speech. Our God is Creator of heaven and earth and everything in between. We need

---

[2] *Harmatia*, BDAG 50-51.
[3] *Exousia*, BDAG 352-353, meanings 4 and 6.
[4] Aēr, BDAG 23, 2b.

not cede the atmosphere to Satan and his minions; he is a usurper of God's creation, not its rightful resident.

In our deadness, we mindlessly follow the value systems of the culture around us – "the *ways* of this world" (NIV) or "*course* of this world" (KJV, NRSV).[5] Oh, we don't admit to mindlessly following, and we do so in a very deliberate, individualistic, self-deterministic way, but we have absorbed the self-centered, relativistic values of our culture, and can't help but express those.

What is really scary, however, is that in our deadness we end up following Satan, "the ruler[6] of the kingdom of the air," who is the great Deceiver. In our deadness we lack discernment. Our lives are filled with the cravings of our sinful nature (vs. 3) – desires, lusts, thoughts, jealousy, envy, strife, selfishness, you name it – which the Tempter inflames. Elsewhere, Paul writes:

> "Don't you know that when you offer yourselves to someone to obey him as slaves, you are slaves to the one whom you obey – whether you are slaves to sin, which leads to death, or to obedience, which leads to righteousness?" (Romans 6:16)

We live in the myth of neutrality. We're not following, we're leading, we tell ourselves. We make our own decisions, we insist. But we are not spiritually powerful enough to lead in this unseen "heavenly realm." We end up being led, duped, victimized, usually without our even knowing it. Our lack of commitment in itself is a commitment, a commitment to follow our whims, and the Tempter is a master of subverting selfish whims.

Verse 3 uses the word *sarx*, "flesh," referring to the "cravings of our sinful nature" (NIV) or the "lusts of our flesh" (KJV). The Greek word *sarx* is used in several senses in the New Testament: (1) literally, the skin and muscles covering our bones; (2) the body itself; (3) the human or mortal nature, then mankind, the "world" as it stands opposed to God; and (4) especially in Paul's letters, "sinful, fallen human nature."[7]

Children of Wrath (2:3b)

> "All of us also lived among them at one time, gratifying the cravings of our sinful nature and following its desires and thoughts. Like the rest, we were by nature objects of wrath." (2:3)

---

[5] *Aiōn*, "age," then "the world as a spatial concert," then perhaps Aeon as a person (BDAG 32-33). But here it probably carries the idea of "world-age" (O'Brien 158-159).

[6] *Archōn*, "ruler, lord, prince," here a transcendent figures such as evil spirits, the devil" (BDAG 140).

[7] *Sarx*, BDAG 914-916.

The wrath of God is another of those counter-cultural concepts. We don't like judgment or judgmentalism in our relativistic society. We have gutted the idea of penal justice to exclude retribution, and are left with a rehabilitative incarceration which fails more often than not, or a society-protective incarceration which produces guilt in us for locking up so many people.

But you can't read the Bible very long until you run smack into the judgment of the righteous God. I hate all that Old Testament judgment and hell-fire and brimstone, you protest. Just give me Jesus and his love.

Have you ever read Jesus' teachings carefully? He talks more about hell and judgment than anyone else in the New Testament. We can't escape it. There's no dichotomy between the Old and New Testament God. Our God is a God who insists on justice and its consequent judgment. And if we try to live free of God's absolute law we become "objects of wrath" like the rest of mankind.

This passage calls those without God "children" (NIV, KJV) or "objects"[8] (NIV) of wrath in this case, a common characteristic of being subject to God's wrath. "Wrath" (Greek *orgē*) is a "strong indignation directed at wrongdoing, with focus on retribution, wrath.... of God's future judgment, specifically qualified as punitive."[9]

Sinners by Nature (2:3)

Moreover, we are this way "by nature," Greek *physis* (from which we get our word "physical"). It refers to a "condition or circumstance as determined by birth, natural endowment or condition, nature, especially as inherited from one's ancestors, in contrast to status or characteristics that are acquired after birth."[10]

So we are being punished for something that is not our fault? you might ask. No, we are being rescued from something that has overpowered our race and victimized us, and from which we cannot escape without assistance, without a Savior. This is Augustine's concept of "original sin" found clearly in the Scriptures. But "original sin" does not mean that we don't sin. We do – and are responsible for the sins we commit. And because of our sins, we are subject to God's wrath and judgment.

Does God blame us for something we have no control over? No. We do have control over our actions or "free will" has no meaning. But we are weak and break God's holy standards of conduct and righteousness.

[8] *Teknon*, here expresses a Hebrew idiom that refers to "a class of persons with a specific characteristic," BDAG 994-995.

[9] *Orgē*, BDAG 720-721.

[10] *Physis*, BDAG 1069-1070.

In a court of law is a person pronounced "not guilty" because he was ignorant of the law? No. If he was intoxicated and couldn't control his actions? No. Because he claimed he was raised in a difficult environment and shouldn't be blamed? No. Is God fair? Yes, eminently fair. When justice is fair, we lose because we sin – willfully at times – against God's holy law. What we need is not justice or fairness. What we need is mercy and grace. That's all we have left to hang onto.

Verse 4 repeats the judgment of verse 1: " dead in transgressions (*paraptōma*[11])." Our sins have produced a spiritual deadness and dullness in us.

We don't like talking about judgment against sin, do we? So why spend time talking about it? Because it gives us a needed corrective to our culture's willful blindness and sense that we can live independent of God's mercy. And it enables us to really appreciate the gracious gift of God which Paul goes on to explain in the remainder of the passage.

Q2. (Ephesians 2:1-3) Few people would knowingly follow Satan. How can people unwittingly follow Satan? In what sense are we responsible for unwitting rebellion against God? How can God, in all fairness, blame us?
http://www.joyfulheart.com/forums/index.php?showtopic=508

Grace and Mercy (2:4-5)

"But because of his great love for us, God, who is rich in mercy, made us alive with Christ even when we were dead in transgressions – it is by grace you have been saved." (2:4-5)

In the previous sentence, Paul was talking about sin and judgment. Look at these contrasting words:

- "God, who is rich in **mercy**."
- "God ... who **made** us **alive** with Christ."
- "It is by **grace** you have been saved."

In the next chapter in this study we'll examine God's grace in detail. But here let's get acquainted with some of the words and their meanings:

---

[11] *Paraptōma* uses an imagery of making a false step so as to lose footing, "a violation of moral standards, offense, wrongdoing, sin" (BDAG 770, bγ).

"Mercy" (Greek *eleos*) means "kindness or concern expressed for someone in need, compassion, mercy, pity, clemency."[12]

"Grace" (Greek *charis*) means literally "favor ... a beneficent disposition toward someone, grace, gracious help, good will."[13] It describes one's attitude toward another which is unilateral, that is, one-sided, not depending upon what another does. "Grace" is not about merit or deserving, but about an unexplained love and generosity and giving on the part of the shower of that favor. Perhaps the best short definition of "grace" is "unmerited favor."

God has given us freely what we absolutely do not deserve. But notice, that this is not a new revelation of God. It amplifies the ancient revelation to Moses:

> "The LORD, the LORD, the compassionate and gracious God, slow to anger, abounding in love and faithfulness, maintaining love to thousands, and forgiving wickedness, rebellion and sin...." (Exodus 34:6-7)

Nor is this an isolated quotation, but is repeated again and again and again throughout the so-called "judgmental" Old Testament: Numbers 14:18; Nehemiah 9:17; Psalm 86:15; Psalm 103:8; Psalm 145:8; Joel 2:13; Jonah 4:2; and Nahum 1:3.

Our rich-in-mercy God has struck again. This time where we have no basis at all of deserving mercy, he has taken the judgment we deserved upon himself in order to spare us. While we were dead ... he made us alive, an echo from Romans:

> "You see, at just the right time, when we were still powerless, Christ died for the ungodly. Very rarely will anyone die for a righteous man, though for a good man someone might possibly dare to die. But God demonstrates his own love for us in this: While we were still sinners, Christ died for us." (Romans 5:6-8)

The apostle Peter reinforces this truth:

> "For Christ died for sins once for all, the righteous for the unrighteous, to bring you to God" (1 Peter 3:18a)

Coming back to our passage in Ephesians 2:5, Paul sums it up: "It is by grace you have been saved." Think once more about grace. It is favor which resides in heart of the grace-giver, not in a reaction to the action or non-action of the recipient. It is unilateral, one-sided favor which isn't dependent upon our deeds. It is "while-we-were-yet-sinners" favor. There's no other explanation for it. God's favor in Jesus Christ is neither earned or deserved. It just *is*.

---

[12] *Eleos*, BDAG 316.
[13] *Charis*, BDAG 1079-1081.

Q3. (Ephesians 1:4-5) In verses 4 and 5, which words describe God's motivation and character? Which verbs describe what has happened to us in Christ?
http://www.joyfulheart.com/forums/index.php?showtopic=509

Seated with Christ in Heavenly Realms (2:6)

> "And God raised us up with Christ and seated us with him in the heavenly realms in Christ Jesus...." (2:6)

Greek is full of compound words. We see three such words in verses 4-6, each containing as a prefix the preposition *syn-* which is a "marker of accompaniment and association,"[14] "together with" or "along with."

- *Syzoōpoieō* (*syn* + *zoō*, "alive" + *poieō*, "make"), "make alive together with someone"[15] (2:4). See also Colossians 2:13.
- *Synegeirō* (*syn* + *egeirō*, "awaken, lift up"), "cause someone to awaken or to rise up with another"[16] (2:4). See also at Colossians 2:12; 3:1.
- *Sygkathizō* (*syn* + *kathizō*), "cause to sit down with someone"[17] (2:6).

These words assume our union with Christ so that his action is our action, since we are in him.

God's grace is more than forgiveness of the past, it is the equipping to live now – in the present time – with new power, power to transform our lives and the lives of those around us.

> "And God raised us up with Christ and seated us with him in the heavenly realms in Christ Jesus ..." (vs. 6)

You'll notice in Ephesians 1:20-22, Jesus is exalted to the right hand of the Father "in the heavenly realms," far above all demonic and human authorities and powers, with everything "under his feet." So, if we are seated "with him in the heavenly realms" then we are elevated above the demonic and human authorities in this spiritual sense. Instead of being victimized by the enemy, we can exercise spiritual authority – when we learn

---

[14] *Syn*, BDAG 961-963.
[15] *Syzoōpoieō*, BDAG 954-955.
[16] *Synegeirō*, BGAD 967.
[17] *Sygkathizō*, BDAG 951.

our place of authority, and learn how to exercise it – *over* the enemy and make him the victim of Christ's victory again and again.

Surely, this is what this passage is intended to mean!

But the typical Christian is blind to his place of authority and power in the heavenly realms, oblivious to promises of answered prayer, with the "eyes of his heart" blinded and blinder-ed. That is why in 1:18-19 Paul prays for the Ephesians for revelation of their true hope, their true inheritance, their true power. We can't see this except by revelation from God. But, thankfully, God desires to reveal it to us.

Q4. (Ephesians 2:6) What does it mean that we are seated with Christ in "the heavenly realms"? What does this say about God's grace? What does this say about our spiritual authority? How should this knowledge affect our prayers and our boldness?
http://www.joyfulheart.com/forums/index.php?showtopic=510

Ages of Grace (2:7)

Paul's soliloquy closes with God's great plan for us for "the coming ages":

"… in order that in the coming ages he might show the incomparable riches of his grace, expressed in his kindness to us in Christ Jesus." (2:7)

God's love isn't just to "get us saved," but to continue to shower us with his love and blessings forever and ever, world without end. Amen.

We started the chapter with bad news of man's blind following of the spirit of the age – and of Satan himself – into spiritually-deadly "transgressions and sins" and "wrath." Not a pretty picture. But without hardly drawing a breath, Paul continues to contrast our fallen human state with our exalted grace-filled state of forgiveness and rescue, of spiritual power and authority, of long heaven-summer-days of basking in our Father's wonderful riches for us. I can't think of much better news than that!

Prayer

Father, we thank you for your incredible, undeserved love and forgiveness. What a gift to us! All we can say is "thank you." All we can do is kneel in surrender and rise to serve you. We love you. In Jesus' awesome name, "God saves," we pray. Amen.

Key Verses

"But because of his great love for us, God, who is rich in mercy, [5]made us alive with Christ even when we were dead in transgressions – it is by grace you have been saved." (Ephesians 2:4-5)

"And God raised us up with Christ and seated us with him in the heavenly realms in Christ Jesus." (Ephesians 2:6)

5. Salvation By Grace Through Faith (2:8-10)

Ephesians 2:8-9 is probably the clearest expression of the basis of our relationship with God found anywhere in the Bible. But to understand it we need to examine some pretty heavy theological concepts.

The Need for a Rescue Operation

> "For it is by grace you have been **saved**, through faith" (2:8a)

First, let's look at salvation, "saved" (*sōzō*). We can understand it best when we strip it for a moment of all of its religious connotations

The best example of utter grace in the Bible is Jesus' parable of the prodigal son. Detail from Rembrandt van Rijn (Dutch painter, 1606-1669), "The Return of the Prodigal Son" (1636), etching on laid paper, plate: 15.6 x 13.7 cm, National Gallery of Art, Washington, DC.

and look at its root meaning: "rescue." Salvation means rescuing someone from a situation that put them in danger or would have been fatal if they had not been removed from it. Salvation is rescuing us from our condition, spelled out earlier in the chapter in 2:1-4:

1. **Spiritual deadness** (2:1) is caused by transgressions and sin. Whereas we might have been open to spiritual things once, able to immediately and intuitively understand them and enter into them, our repeated sins and transgressions of God's holy principles has somehow dulled us, deadened us, so we are unperceptive. We are without spiritual life as it pertains to God.

2. **Followers of our corrupt culture**, followers of "the ways of this world" (2:2a). No matter how counter-culture we may think we are, in actuality, we have absorbed the spirit of the age. We have internalized its corrupt values and jaded outlook.

3. **Followers of Satan**, "the ruler of the kingdom of the air" (2:2b). Though we may not be deliberate Satan worshippers, we have become dupes, unknowing adherents to a pride and attitude toward God that has its origins in the rebellious Snake himself (Genesis 3:1-7). We respond readily enough to his tempting whispers and think of them our own thoughts. Though we pretend an independence of direction, we have come under his influence and are now marching to his drumbeat.

4. **Self-indulgent,** "gratifying the cravings of our sinful nature and following its desires and thoughts" (2:3a). We desire, we want, we burn with lust, with hate, with greed, and we steal to satisfy ourselves. Our self-centeredness becomes self-destructiveness. We are spiraling, winding about ourselves, the tether getting shorter and shorter as it raps around the central pole, until we turn inward to an emptiness that is the internal symptom of spiritual deadness.

5. **Under Divine judgment and righteous anger** (2:3b). No matter how much God loves us – and he does with all his heart – there is that part of him which is the epitome of justice and fairness which recognizes our rebellion and spiritual treason for what it is and passes judgment on us and our sins. We are loved, but under a sentence of death. We are rebels awaiting our final day in court before the Great White Throne judgment of God (Revelation 20:11-15) when our sentence will be executed upon us.

Only when seen in stark relief against the dark backdrop of our predicament, does God's love shine with all its brilliance. We don't deserve God's favor. We are like children straining to leave home, having resisted his thoughts and directions and tender care. We have turned to ourselves like overgrown children, delinquents now to be judged as adults in criminal court.

Results of Rescue (2:4-6)

Now look at the rapid succession of blessings in our passage:

1. His great **love** for us (2:4a).
2. His richness of **mercy** (2:4b).
3. A miracle of **new birth** ("alive together with Christ") in the place of our terminal spiritual deadness ("dead in transgressions" (2:5).

4. Elevation to a spiritual authority and **position** "in the heavenly realms" far above that of our tempter and his minions – at the very right hand of God with Christ our Messiah (2:6).

5. Eternal **kindness** shown us forever and ever, on and on, extending into the far reaches of eternity, Christ delights in showing us kindness (2:7).

Contrast what we deserve with what we have been given and you see grace in all clarity.

"Grace" Is More than a Girl's Name

"For it is by grace you have been saved, through faith...." (2:8a)

The word "grace" as we discussed in a previous chapter, was not at first a theological word. Greek *charis* means simply "favor."[1] To show grace is to bestow favor. Notice carefully, it has nothing to do with reward for "good behavior." The benefactor doesn't show favor because we have earned it, but simply because he wants to. He is under no obligation to love because we have somehow driven him to it. He just loves. The impetus for the favor is entirely the prerogative of the giver, like a great aunt who delights to send things to her nieces and nephews even though they neglect to write and thank her.

"I've been a good boy, so I deserve a lot of presents under the tree this year." This is not a good boy speaking, but a spoiled brat who wants to subvert the spirit of the season to his own selfishness. God isn't some celestial Santa Claus, "making a list and checking it twice, trying to find out who's naughty or nice." That view of Christmas was invented by manipulative parents trying to leverage the holiday to induce good behavior.

We grossly misunderstand God's favor if we see it as wages or rewards – that would be justice not grace. This is gift-giving, pure and simple. Like the runner to first base who knows he didn't quite make it, but the base umpire lifts his hands and shouts out "Safe!" "That was a gift," mutters the first baseman under his breath. Yes, our "safeness" is a gift, not our due. We were "out." We missed it. We've been rescued from what is our due.

When we like someone, we want to send flowers, shower upon them expressions of our love. Cards, presents, unexpected gifts. Please open it. Now? Yes, I just want to see

---

[1] *Charis*, "a beneficent disposition toward someone, favor, grace, gracious care/help, goodwill (almost a technical term in the reciprocity-oriented world dominated by Hellenic influence). Active, that which one grants to another, the action of one who volunteers to do something not otherwise obligatory." (BDAG 1079-1081, 2a).

the expression of delight upon your face. The great abandon of favor which exists on its own terms and not ours. Grace and gift-giving go hand in hand, undeserved, given out of love and favor.

Q1. Why is it so hard for us to understand grace? What commonly held life principle does it demolish? Translate the word "grace" into language a 10-year-old child would understand.
http://www.joyfulheart.com/forums/index.php?showtopic=511

"Saved" is the Greek verb *sōzō*, while "salvation is the noun *sōteria*. In classical Greek "both the verb and the noun denote rescue and deliverance in the sense of averting some danger threatening life. This can happen in war or at sea. But that which one is delivered from may also be an illness. Where no immediate danger is mentioned, they can mean to keep or preserve."[2] When speaking to non-Christians (and Christians, too, for that matter) I often substitute the word "rescued" for "saved," since that word is processed by the hearer in its normal rather than Christian-jargon sense.

Q2. "Saved" has become Christian jargon. How can you "translate" this word into modern speech so people can understand what it really means and why they need it?
http://www.joyfulheart.com/forums/index.php?showtopic=512

So we've examined the ideas of rescue (salvation) and God's inexplicable but very real favor towards us (grace). Now we need to look at "works."

Working Our Way into the Good Graces of God (2:9)

> "For it is by grace you have been saved, through faith – and this not from yourselves, it is the gift of God – not by works, so that no one can boast." (2:8-9)

Paul was raised a strict Pharisee, whose highest value was exact and minute obedience to the Torah, God's law. If he obeyed then he was righteous. If he disobeyed he then he was unrighteous. It was black or white. The Judaism of Jesus' and Paul's day

---

[2] Colin Brown, "Redemption," *New International Dictionary of New Testament Theology* (NIDNTT), 3:205ff. *Sōzō*, "to preserve or rescue from dangers and afflictions, save, keep from harm, rescue." Here transcendent danger or destruction is in view: save, preserve from eternal death" (BDAG 982-983).

had reduced the principles of God's law into inflexible and sometimes petty rules. The rules are a "hedge" around the law, the Torah. Keep the petty rules, they reasoned, and you are prevented from breaking the actual law. That was Phariseeism, prompted by a desire to obey God.

But eventually they mistook the petty rules for the law. Don't say "God" because you might take his name in vain, so you substitute "heaven" for God and you're safe. When God's name appears in the sacred text as *Yahweh*, you pronounce it as if it said "Lord" (*Adonai*).

A minor verse in the law said, "Do not cook a young goat in its mother's milk," obviously intended to instill some sense of mercy towards the animals one was butchering for food (Exodus 23:19b). Judaism turned it into a system of keeping a Kosher kitchen with one set of pots and pans used for dairy products, and a completely different set used for meat products, lest they inadvertently boil a kid in its mother's milk. You get the idea.

A Self-Serving Righteousness

Paul's Judaism had degenerated from faithfulness to God's principles to strict and blind adherence to man-made rules. Then it elevated obedience to these man-made rules into a system of earned righteousness before God. By their right actions they put God in their debt. Never mind that their hearts were still self-centered and self-serving. Never mind that they lived their whole lives to save themselves. They were righteous. That was what counted. When Paul says in Ephesians 2:9 that you have been saved "not by works (*ergon*), so that no one can boast," this is what he is talking about.

Paul the Christian gives up "a righteousness of my own that comes from the law" (Philippians 3:9), and instead embraces "the righteousness that comes from God and is by faith."

Paul the Christian isn't lawless, but he has finally come to understand that God's favor isn't earned by surface observance of religious rules. He has come to understand the darkness and dullness of his own heart. He, who had gone to Damascus to imprison followers of Jesus, had himself been arrested by this Jesus (Acts 9). He, the righteous murderer of Christians, had received mercy from the hand of the One whom he was persecuting. He now understands the emptiness of a religion based on outward rules while fostering an inward self-centered rather than God-centered motivation.

The Just Shall Live by Their Faith

Paul rejects this kind of works-based righteousness in favor of a gift-based righteousness, which is received by faith – that is, simple trust, simple acceptance that believes at face value that God loves you – faith that puts out its open hand to receive, and says thank you to the Giver when it has taken hold of the gift.

Israel's founding fathers had lived by this kind of simple receiving of God's blessings from the very beginning, Paul realizes. He announces, "The just shall live by faith" (Romans 1:17), quoting from Habakkuk 2:4. It wasn't Abraham's worthiness that saved him, but God's favor that made him worthy and brought out the very best in him (Genesis 15:6).

We see in our Ephesians passage a radical statement of the roots of our religion. We are saved by God's favor. Period. Not by our own goodness.

"Faith" is another word that has degenerated into Christian jargon. In classical Greek, *pistis* means "the trust that a man may place in men or the gods, credibility, credit in business, guarantee, proof, or something entrusted."[3]

Our society is plagued by "easy believism." "Oh, of course, I believe in God," really means, "I acknowledge that there is a Supreme Being." That's an important step from atheism or agnosticism, but it is not faith. "You believe that there is one God. Good! Even the demons believe that – and shudder" (James 2:19).

The basic concept of Christian faith or belief is "trust," having enough confidence in God to be willing to rely on Him. Of course, it is easily possible to have faith in some aspects of God's provision for us and not others. So there is much room to grow in our knowledge and trust – or to persist in various degrees of unbelief.

If You're Good Enough You Can Go to Heaven

American religious mythology communicates just the opposite. Simply stated it goes like this: If you're good you'll go to heaven. If you're bad you'll go to hell. Of course, we're not bad enough to go to hell, we say nervously. We've been generous (sometimes), we've been good neighbors (at least the times we remember), we haven't beaten our wives (with our fists). We are basically good people and so a fair-minded God will send us to heaven when we die. Won't he? Of course he will, dear.

Our culture, you see, doesn't understand a gift-righteousness, only a works-righteousness. We can justify ourselves only by means of a befuddled mind that ignores our real spiritual condition: spiritual deadness, self-centeredness, and an adoption of the

[3] Otto Michel, "Faith," NIDNTT 1:594.

world's (and ultimately Satan's) perverted values. A works-righteousness puts *us* in control; a gift-righteousness makes us utterly dependent upon the Giver, something that our lack of trust – lack of faith, in reality – makes us shun.

By now we've talked about what "works" is referring to. But to be complete, we need to talk about what it does *not* mean. For that we turn to James chapter 2.

The Essential Marriage of Faith and Works

"... Faith by itself, if it is not accompanied by action (works, KJV) is dead" (James 2:17)

The word "works," Greek *ergon*, in classical Greek referred to "a deed, an action, by contrast either with inactivity or a mere word."[4] This is the sense in which James uses the word.

However, Paul uses the word in a technical sense:

"In Judaism ... the view of works necessary for the fulfillment of the law and therefore for righteousness is developed and consolidated. The way to godliness is casuistically prescribed for the Jew by a multiplicity of regulations for the performance of the law."[5]

As mentioned above, Paul's background as a Pharisee (Philippians 3:4-6) had led him to believe that if he acted righteously enough he could merit salvation. Today's strict Hasidic Jews are the spiritual descendents of the Pharisees. They believe they will be saved by their strict adherence to the 613 commandments in the Torah. Paul firmly rejects this view.

Whereas Paul is coming from a Pharisaical understanding of the idea of "works" meriting favor in the eyes of God, James uses the same word "works" but by it means something entirely different: deeds, actions.

James writes in response to people who had perverted salvation by grace into "it doesn't matter how you live or what you do, you're saved anyway."

James' point is this: Saying you have faith isn't enough. Your faith needs to be evidenced in your actions, your deeds, your lifestyle. If it isn't, it probably isn't genuine faith. If it isn't, you're probably kidding yourself about really trusting God with your life. James isn't saying that our deeds save us. He doesn't even come close. He is saying that if our faith hasn't affected our lives, then it probably isn't real but "dead."

While we see a verbal contradiction here – they both use the same word "works" – I don't think Paul would disagree in the least. Paul, however, is clarifying grace-based

---

[4] Hans-Christoph Hahn, "Work," NIDNTT 3:1147, *ergon*.

[5] NIDNTT 3:1149. "... of the deeds of humans, exhibiting a consistent moral character, referred to collectively as 'works'" (BDAG 390-391, 1cβ).

salvation in the face of a pervasive works-based understanding of salvation prevalent in the Judaism of his time. James is trying to help Christians own up to their own self-deception about their spiritual condition, a sterile "faith" that is vapor, a "faith" which doesn't change the person.

The Cart Comes after the Horse

Works follow faith, not the other way around. Of course, we don't change everything overnight. Our character took 15 or 20 or 30 or 40 years to get to where it is, and it takes God's Spirit a while to form in us the character of Christ. Don't berate yourself because you see areas of sin in you that Christ has not yet softened and lifted out of you. Our salvation springs from God's gift, and is consummated by our trusting acceptance ("through faith"). It is *after* salvation has been received that God begins his real work in us, not before. It is as a *result* of salvation that we begin to produce actions, which reflect our faith. James says it this way: "Faith without works is dead."

Working Out our Destiny (2:10)

Paul says it a different way in our passage:

> "For we are God's workmanship (a gift), created in Christ Jesus to do good works (the result of our faith-response to God), which God prepared in advance for us to do." (2:10)

Faith-energized works are our destiny!

The word "prepared in advance" (NIV) or "before ordained" (KJV) in vs. 10 is the Greek verb *prohetoimazo, pro-*, "before" + *hetoimazō*, "get ready, hold in readiness."[6]

God planned for us before we were even born to do special "good works." The scripture says he "prepared in advance" for us to do them. I take this to mean that we have been prepared in advance by having been given particular aptitudes, special spiritual sensitivies, unique abilities – "spiritual gifts," if you will – which equip or prepare us to fulfill our destiny here on earth (and, who knows, maybe in the Kingdom beyond, also).

Q3. According to Ephesians 2:10, what were we created to do? Why? (Matthew 5:16) What is the difference between these works and the works Paul discredits in verse 9?
http://www.joyfulheart.com/forums/index.php?showtopic=513

---

[6] Siegfried Solle, "Ready, Prepare, Gird," NIDNTT 3:116-118.

This Not of Yourselves

"For it is by grace you have been saved, through faith – and this not from yourselves, it is the gift of God – [9]not by works, so that no one can boast." (2:8-9)

By now we've looked at each of the important concepts contained in this classic passage, Ephesians 2:8-10, except for one: "and this not from yourselves, it is the gift of God" (2:8b). Okay, Paul, exactly which thing is the gift here? Let's look at the candidates: grace, salvation, and faith. The phrase "and this not from yourselves" could refer grammatically to any or all of them. This what?

This grace is certainly not from us. It is the generous gift of the Giver, given against all odds, against all of our self-centered, rebellious history. Grace is certainly not from ourselves.

This salvation? The rescue operation, which culminated in the cross, was launched by the Father with the willing cooperation of his Son Jesus. We had nothing to do with it that we can boast about. Unless we can boast about uttering a feeble "Help" at some point when we were acutely aware of the desperateness of our plight. Certainly the rescue, the salvation, is not from ourselves.

This faith? Faith is certainly something which comes from us, isn't it? Well, the best we can say is "sort of." The New Testament is filled with what John Wesley called "prevenient grace," grace which comes before, grace which precedes the actual event of our salvation. "You are the Christ, the Son of the Living God," exclaimed Peter. "This wasn't revealed to you by man," Jesus retorted, "but by my Father in heaven" (Matthew 16:16-17). Peter's faith-insight into Jesus' true nature was a God-given revelation, not from himself so that Peter could boast. "No one can come to me unless the Father who sent me draws him," Jesus said (John 6:44). So our faith is in response to the Father's gentle drawing, the Holy Spirit's persistent conviction that we are sinful (John 16:8-11). We can't take credit for our faith, either.

Most recent commentators see "this not from yourselves" as referring to salvation by grace as a whole, including faith.[7]

Q4. What exactly is faith? Can we take credit for having it? Can we be condemned for lacking it? Define "faith" in terms a 10-year-old could understand.
http://www.joyfulheart.com/forums/index.php?showtopic=514

---

[7] O'Brien 175, fn. 91.

Influence without Coercion

But at this point I have to depart from those who teach "irresistible grace." While God assists us towards himself, he does not compel us against our will. He increases our understanding, he heightens our sense of need, he softens our will. Yes, I'll grant you all of that. But there is still a place where we are required to assent to him as an act of our own will, a free response to God's unconditional love. A "decision," as Billy Graham would call it.

Can we take credit for the decision? Boast about it? Of course not. That would be like a starving man boasting about going up to get a loaf of bread after hearing where the bread-line is to be found. While one important *element* of our faith is a free-will decision to say "yes" to the Master, it is only an element, and not one we can boast of. The other elements are knowledge (given by revelation), conviction (brought by the Holy Spirit), occasion (planned in advance by God), and doubtless others as well.

So, coming back to our question from Ephesians 2:9. "And this not of yourselves, it is the gift of God." What does "this" refer to? Salvation, grace, or faith? I would have to answer, "Yes, all of the above." All three are gracious gifts from God for which we can take no credit.

Paraphrase

Let's conclude these rich verses with a paraphrase that sums up what the verses mean:

We were dead to God spiritually, our wills turned inward to follow our own desires, ready dupes for the great Tempter. We were under God's righteous judgment, no denying it. "But God" who is "rich in mercy" acted out of his own heart of love and bestowed upon us his gracious favor – no credit to us here – which rescued us from ourselves, and from Satan, and from the pull of the world, and set us on a new path. A path which is determined to receive random acts of kindness from God unto all eternity, as we fulfill our destiny to do good works for which God has specifically and individually equipped us – true significance for the present and for the future, world without end. Amen.

Prayer

Father, without your persistent grace towards us we would be truly lost and wandering far from you. But you have had mercy on our souls. You have wooed us, drawn us, and then enwrapped us in your arms. Thank you. Thank you. In Jesus' name, we thank you. Amen.

Key Verses

"[8]For it is by grace you have been saved, through faith–and this not from yourselves, it is the gift of God– [9]not by works, so that no one can boast. [10]For we are God's workmanship, created in Christ Jesus to do good works, which God prepared in advance for us to do." (Ephesians 2:8-10)

6. Fellow Citizens with the People of God (2:11-22)

In the summers of my college years I worked in a factory in Oakland, California. Compared to the grizzled old workers who had spent a lifetime in that place, I was just an upstart. I would just be there for a summer or two and they didn't spend much time getting to know me. I was tolerated, even occasionally appreciated, but that was as far as it went. I was the outsider and never made it inside.

If you've ever moved to a new community or entered a school-room where you didn't know a soul, then you know a little of what Gentile Christians must have felt like in a congregation dominated by those whose families had been Jewish from time immemorial. In Ephesians 2:11-22, Paul recalls this sense of apartness, and writes with the intention of helping Gentile

The lion shall lie down with the lamb in Messiah's Kingdom, Isaiah prophesied (Isaiah 11:6). Detail from Edward Hicks (American Quaker painter, 1780-1849), "The Peaceable Kingdom" (c. 1834), oil on canvas, 74.5x90.1 cm., National Gallery of Art, Washington DC.

Christians – and Jewish Christians – to understand their essential oneness in Jesus Christ.

Separated from Christ (2:11-12)

> "Therefore, remember that formerly you who are Gentiles by birth and called "uncircumcised" by those who call themselves "the circumcision" (that done in the body by the hands of men) – remember that at that time you were separate from Christ, excluded from citizenship in Israel and foreigners to the covenants of the promise, without hope and without God in the world." (2:11-12)

Paul begins by listing the elements of the Gentiles' spiritual condition pre-Christ:

- **Uncircumcised**, lacking that ancient mark of being part of the Covenant Family of God;
- **Separate from Christ**, utterly cut off from the Messiah;
- **Excluded from citizenship** among the people of God, aliens;
- **Foreigners to the covenants** made to Abraham, Isaac, Jacob, and Moses, which tied the people to God with responsibilities and gave them wonderful promises;
- **Without hope** or certainty or promise for the present, or for the future; and
- **Without God** in the world.

Pretty depressing. The phrase "with hope and without God in the world" echoes in my head as describing utter aloneness. Many of our friends and neighbors, co-workers and relatives could be described by these words. Maybe you, too, feel this way. A person who is not united to God through Christ is alone, is lost, is without hope.

We who know Christ have really Good News to share with people who are sometimes acutely aware of their loneliness. For people longing to belong, we offer inclusion into a loving family.

Q1. (Ephesians 2:11-12) Why does being out of touch with what it means to be "lost" impede our willingness to witness? In your own words, what is the spiritual condition of a friend or co-worker who doesn't know Christ?
http://www.joyfulheart.com/forums/index.php?showtopic=515

When people who are estranged come back together we call it "being reconciled." That is what Christ did for us who were far away from God: he brought us back to God. This passage spells it out in detail.

Brought Near through His Blood (2:13)

"But now in Christ Jesus you who once were far away have been brought near through the blood of Christ." (2:13)

"Brought near through the blood of Christ" is really a kind of shorthand to describe the process of our redemption. I want to explore this more fully, since the requirements of the Jewish sacrificial system described in the law of Moses fourteen centuries before Christ were fulfilled in this redemption. (You'll find these regulations delineated in Exodus and Leviticus.)

God is a holy God, and requires righteousness and moral holiness in the lives of his people. To teach holiness to his people after their deliverance from Egypt, God had them set up a tabernacle in the wilderness surrounded by a curtained-off courtyard. The common people could not approach God's dwelling place in a casual manner; they brought with them a sacrifice, confessing their sins while laying their hands on the head of the animal sacrifice. Before their eyes the animal was killed in their stead, for their sins, and its blood sprinkled on the altar where part of the sacrifice was burned (Leviticus 4).

Only the priests could enter the tabernacle to care for the holy things, and only the high priest could enter the Holy of Holies, the "throne room" of God where the Ark of the Covenant was placed, and then only once a year on the Day of Atonement for the sins of the people (Leviticus 16).

When Paul wrote that we have been "brought near through the blood of Christ," he means that Christ the Messiah has become the sacrifice for our sins, and because of his death on our behalf, we can approach God with our sins forgiven.

Completing the Law's Requirements (2:14-15)

> "For he himself is our peace, who has made the two one and has destroyed the barrier, the dividing wall of hostility, by abolishing in his flesh the law with its commandments and regulations. His purpose was to create in himself one new man out of the two, thus making peace…" (2:14-15)

In Hebrew the word *shālōm* can mean "completion and fulfillment – of entering into a state of wholeness and unity, a restored relationship."[1] It carries the ideas of peace, wholeness, wholesomeness, reconciliation, blessing, restoration. It is a very wonderful and broad word. Paul says in 2:14 that Christ himself is our peace, our Shalom, our healing and wholeness, and the one who brought an end to the tension between us and God, which our sin had created.

But this Shalom was brought about by what we call today a "paradigm shift," a "sea change," a basic alteration in the whole way God was dealing with man. Prior to Christ the Law was the barrier between Jew and Gentile. The Jews kept it rigorously, the Gentiles disregarded it. It had become a dividing wall between them: a source of pride to the Jews, an object of scorn to the Gentiles. Look at the finality of these words:

> "He … has destroyed (*luō*) the barrier … by abolishing (*kartargeō*) in his flesh the law with its commandments and ordinances" (2:14-15)

[1] G. Lloyd Carr, *shālēm*, TWOT #2401a.

The word translated "abolishing, abolished" is Greek *katargeō* (from *kata*, "separation, dissolution," + *argeō*, "to be idle, inactive"). It means "to cause something to lose its power or effectiveness, invalidate, make powerless," then "to cause something to come to an end or to be no longer in existence, abolish, wipe out, set aside something."[2]

Wow! When Jesus had been accused of abolishing the commandments, he had said:

> "I have not come to abolish them but to fulfill them. I tell you the truth, until heaven and earth disappear, not the smallest letter, not the least stroke of a pen, will by any means disappear from the Law until everything is accomplished" (Matthew 5:17-18)

Moral, Ceremonial, and Civil Law

One way of looking at the Law in the Old Testament is as three basic components:

1. **The moral law**, the enduring principles of righteousness which are timeless, such as the Ten Commandments.
2. **The ceremonial law**, pertaining to the tabernacle, temple, priests, and sacrifices.
3. **The civil law**, rules concerning property, crime, and punishment.

1. Moral Law

The moral law, of course, is woven into the fabric of the creation. It cannot be done away with any more than righteousness can become obsolete. But it was fulfilled completely in Jesus Christ, the perfect, sinless man who lived the life of God before us in the flesh.

2. Ceremonial Law

As we have seen above, Jesus fulfilled the ceremonial law, which prescribed how sin was to be forgiven, and who should gain admittance to the Holiest of Holy Places, the very Presence of God. Jesus was the ultimate sacrifice for the sins of each of us. In the Old Testament, God permitted a lesser (an animal) to substitute or stand in for the punishment deserved by the greater (a sinful man). In the New Testament, the greater (God's very Son) became the substitute or stand in for the punishment deserved by the lesser (all men). In his own body, with his own blood, for all time, Jesus fulfilled the whole of the ceremonial law. When he died, the veil of the temple, separating people from the holy place of God, was rent in two from top to bottom (Matthew 27:51), signifying that God had opened up the way to his very Presence through the Messiah.

---

[2] *Katargeō*, BDAG 525-526.

After Jesus, temple sacrifices became superfluous. Every time an animal was sacrificed for sin after the Lamb of God had made the ultimate sacrifice, it was a kind of hollow mockery of what Christ had done. As the writer of Hebrews said, the Old Covenant is now "obsolete" (NIV, NRSV, Hebrews 8:13).[3] Jesus fulfilled the religious, ceremonial law, and by completing it, rendered it obsolete.

3. Civil Law

The civil law, too, had been fulfilled when the Messiah came and the Old Covenant became obsolete. Its time was past. God had been Israel's King in the Wilderness. When the people had clamored for a king, God gave them Saul, and then David. But Israel's last king, last "son of David," had been taken into exile in 587 BC. Now in Jesus Christ, the "Son of David," "the Son of God," the ultimate King of the Jews had come. Heralded by angels and sought as King by wise men at his birth, Jesus had finally stood before Pontius Pilate and acknowledged that his Kingship was "not of this world."

Q2. (Ephesians 2:14-15) In what sense did Jesus as Messiah "fulfill" the Mosaic Law? What is the significance of that for Jewish people? For us Gentiles?
http://www.joyfulheart.com/forums/index.php?showtopic=516

Jew and Gentile as the "New Israel"

The Messiah also decreed the end of the Jewish monopoly as the exclusive people of God: "Therefore I tell you that the Kingdom of God will be taken away from you and given to a people who will produce its fruit" (Matthew 21:43). Now he commanded his followers to "make disciples of all nations" (Matthew 28:19), to "go into all the world and preach the good news to all creation" (Mark 16:15), to "be my witnesses in Jerusalem, and in all Judea and Samaria, and to the ends of the earth" (Acts 1:8). The Gentiles and Jews together became "the Israel of God" (Galatians 6:16). The civil laws intended for the nation of Israel in the Promised Land, while good and useful, had become obsolete as the nation embraced believers throughout the world.

> "... And in this one body to reconcile both of them to God through the cross, by which he put to death their hostility. He came and preached peace to you who were far away and peace to those who were near." (2:16-17)

---

[3] *Palaioō*, "to make old, to declare to be obsolete" (H. Seesemann, *palai, ktl.*, TDNT 5:717-720).

I've spent some time explaining how Jesus "abolished in his flesh the law with its commandments and regulations" (Ephesians 2:15), because this is often misunderstood and disregarded by us Gentile Christians. But know this: for you the Messiah (Christ means "messiah, anointed one," you know) changed his whole plan and now reconciles you to God together with his beloved Jewish people. Instead of treating Gentiles and Jews differently, now they have become in the Messiah "one new man out of the two," ending the Gentile-Jew hostility, "thus making peace" (2:15).

We Christians, who have such a tendency toward pride, division, denominationalism, and separatism from fellow Christians, need to pay special heed. There are two rich words here – "peace" (Greek *eirēnē*, Hebrew *shālōm*), which we examined above, and "reconcile" (*apokatallassō*).[4] Reconciliation happens when an estrangement is healed, a separation is removed. God has reconciled us to himself through Jesus' death on the cross (2 Corinthians 5:19-21).

Access to the Father (2:18)

The next verse contains a wonderful promise:

"For through him we both have access to the Father by one Spirit." (2:18)

Yes, on its face it means that Jew and Gentile are now on equal footing before God.

But I want us to think about the concept of "access" (*prosagōgē*).[5] In the Near East, a monarch's presence was exclusive. Only a few courtiers had the privilege of being with him. If a person had a petition – and he were a citizen – he might have an appointment to bring the need to the king. Non-citizens had no standing whatsoever. No rights. No access. They could write their requests and hope that the king would consider them, but he had no obligation to do so. They were not citizens.

We Christians have a special access to God not granted to others. Yes, they can pray and hope, but they have no privilege. Their prayers are based on hope and desperation. Our prayers are offered "through faith in him" and spring from "freedom and confidence" (Ephesians 3:12).

In our desire to be inclusive and believe in the Brotherhood of Man, we need to realize that Jesus taught an exclusive relationship with God through His Spirit, which results in answered prayer and spiritual power (John 14:12-14; 15:7). The world resists the exclusivity of Christianity and resents it, but it is clearly taught in the Scripture. In

---

[4] *Apokatallassō* means "to change, to exchange, to reconcile" (F. Büchsel, *alassō, ktl.*, TDNT 1:251-259; BDAG 112).

[5] *Prosagōgē*, "way of approach, access" (BDAG 876).

the midst of the now-universal scope of the gospel, people still need to embrace Christ and the gospel with faith to be able to come to God.

Q3. (Ephesians 2:17) What does it mean to have "access to the Father"? In what way does the Holy Spirit facilitate this access? In what way does Jesus enable this access? http://www.joyfulheart.com/forums/index.php?showtopic=517

Made One in Christ (2:18-22)

"¹⁸For through him we both have access to the Father by one Spirit. ¹⁹Consequently, you are no longer foreigners and aliens, but fellow citizens with God's people and members of God's household, ²⁰built on the foundation of the apostles and prophets, with Christ Jesus himself as the chief cornerstone. ²¹In him the whole building is joined together and rises to become a holy temple in the Lord. ²²And in him you too are being built together to become a dwelling in which God lives by his Spirit." (2:18-22)

In contrast to our old place outside of God's blessing and privilege, we now have been given wonderful blessings:

- **Access** to the Father by the Spirit through Christ (a Trinitarian concept)
- **Citizenship** with God's people
- **Family membership** in God's household

Notice that our privileges are *with* God's people, not instead of God's people. All who put their faith in Christ, Jews and Gentiles, are part of the same people of God now.

A Dwelling Place for God in the Spirit (2:22)

"And in him you too are being built together to become a dwelling in which God lives by his Spirit." (2:22)

The final part of this passage contains a play on words in Greek. Verse 19b says we are members of God's house (*oikos*). Both in Greek and in English, the word "house" can mean both "dwelling place" as well as "household." In 2:19, Paul uses the word first with the idea of "household," "fellow citizens with God's people and members of God's household," but then consciously shifts over in 2:20-22 to a related word, "dwelling place" (*katoikētērion*[6]). The dwelling place in this passage is not the individual heart of the believer, but the congregation itself. Our churches are to be "a dwelling place for God" – an awesome thought!

God's "house" is also a "holy temple in the Lord" (2:21) which is spiritual and metaphorical, rather than physical. The apostles and prophets make up the spiritual foundation. Christ is the chief cornerstone which determines and joins together the building. We are perceived as "living stones" (1 Peter 2:4-5) which are "built together" (2:22a).

Notice that the theme is unity with other believers. Some people act as if they were "Lone Ranger" Christians. They isolate themselves from the other believers, don't attend church or support the ministry, and parrot the unscriptural excuse they learned from the world, "You don't have to go to church to be a Christian." As I read Ephesians and the rest of the New Testament, not loving our brothers and sisters enough to get together with them is a mark of non-Christianity. The Apostle John wrote:

> "Dear friends, let us love one another [i.e. other Christian believers], for love comes from God. Everyone who loves has been born of God and knows God. Whoever does not love does not know God, because God is love" (1 John 4:7-8).

The Bible knows no "Lone Ranger" Christians, only believers in fellowship with the other believers in their locality. Yes, there is a place and time for spiritual retreat. Jesus and others drew away for a time of spiritual solitude, fasting, and prayer, but then came back again to be with God's people. Being a perpetual hermit is an aberration, not our command. Our sense of identity according to Ephesians is as part of God's people, part of God's household, stones "being built together" to become a temple.

The Church as a Temple (2:21-22)

> "In him the whole building is joined together and rises to become a holy temple in the Lord. And in him you too are being built together to become a dwelling in which God lives by his Spirit." (2:21-22)

Several times in the New Testament people are spoken of as being a "temple." In 1 Corinthians 6:19 Paul says clearly, "Do you not know that your body is a temple of the Holy Spirit, who is in you, whom you have received from God?" Clearly, he is speaking of the individual Christian here.

---

[6] *Katoikētērion*, "dwelling place" (BDAG 534-535) from *katoikeō*, "to make something a habitation or dwelling by being there, inhabit" (BDAG 434). Also O. Michel, *oikos, ktl.*, TDNT 5:119-159.

But in each of the other instances, the reference to the "temple" is to the church body collectively. 1 Corinthians 3:16-17 warns against destroying the church which has been built by a builder such as Apollos or Paul. 2 Corinthians 6:16-17 is spoken to a people among whom God lives and walks. "We are the temple" rather than "You (singular) are a temple." In 1 Peter 2:4-5 believers are likened to "living stones," which are being built into a spiritual house to be a holy priesthood offering spiritual sacrifices. The context here is clearly of a temple, now with spiritual sacrifices rather than physical ones.

Q4. (Ephesians 2:22) What is the significance that your congregation was made to be "a dwelling place for God in the Spirit"? What hinders that from being fully experienced? What can you do to help that become more fully experienced and appreciated?
http://www.joyfulheart.com/forums/index.php?showtopic=518

Spiritual Masonry

Verses 21 and 22 use three interesting words which describe Jesus' spiritual masonry:

- **"Joined together"** (NIV, NRSV) and "fitly framed together" (KJV) is Greek *synharmologeō*, "fit or join together."[7] This verb is another compound word, with *syn*, "together" + *harmologos*, "binding, joining;" from *harmos*, "a joint," and *legō*, "to lay with." Have you ever laid a brick or stone walkway? Or built a block wall? Then you know how important and exacting the joinery process is.
- **"Grows into"** (NRSV, KJV), "rises to become" (NIV) is Greek *auxanō/auxō*, "become greater, grow, increase."[8]
- **"Built together"** is *synoikodomeō*, "build up (together) or construct various parts,"[9] another compound using *syn*, "together, with" + *oikodomeō*, "to build a house, erect a building."

Ephesians 2:22 has always meant a great deal to me. It says that when Christians gather, we become together a "dwelling place of God in the Spirit" (RSV). There is a special sense in which God meets with his people when they are gathered in his name.

[7] *Synharmologeō*, BDAG 986.
[8] *Auxanō / auxō*, BDAG 151.
[9] *Synoikodomeō*, BDAG 974.

Jesus spoke of the spiritual power of the gathered church: "For where two or three come together in my name, there am I with them" (Matthew 18:20). It's not that he isn't with us as individuals, but that in a very special sense he meets with us when we gather to honor him with brothers and sisters in Christ. I believe that God wishes to fill our gatherings with his presence as powerfully as he did the tabernacle (Exodus 40:34-35) and the temple (1 Kings 8:10-11) when the Shekinah glory of God became so great that the priests could not perform their ministry because of the greatness of the glory of God in his house.

We have been called to be building blocks in a temple, which becomes "the dwelling place of God in the Spirit." From alienation and separateness, we have truly been brought inside God's house to become part of its very structure, to see him in his glory. What a wonderful and high calling!

Prayer

Lord Jesus, bring each of us into the unity for which you lived and died and now intercede before the throne of God. Amen.

Key Verses

"For through him we both have access to the Father by one Spirit." (Ephesians 2:18)

"And in him you too are being built together to become a dwelling in which God lives by his Spirit." (Ephesians 2:22)

: Mystery, Mission, and Ministry of the Church (3:1-

Have you ever had a secret that you didn't tell anyone? A secret that explains your otherwise incomprehensible actions? Perhaps you have. But our secrets tend to be shameful. The secret we're going to study in this passage is anything but that. It is a wonderful secret plan that God has had since the beginning of time and is now ready to reveal. Are you ready?

Detail of St. Paul, Catacombs of Praetextatus, fresco, fourth century.

Exercise: Paul is explaining in the passage the mystery that has surrounded the Gospel. To begin to understand it:

1. **Circle the keywords** "administration," "mystery," and "grace" in the NIV text.

2. Then **Connect the like words** with each other with lines.

If you're using the KJV, "administration" is "dispensation" in verse 2 and "fellowship" in verse 9. In the NRSV it is "commission" in verse 2 and "plan" in verse 9.

Paul the Prisoner (3:1)

"For this reason I, Paul, the prisoner of Christ Jesus for the sake of you Gentiles...." (3:1)

Paul refers back ("for this reason") to what he has just said in 2:11-22, that God has broken down the barrier between the Jews and Gentiles, making Gentile Christians one with God's people, full citizens of the Kingdom of God.

Revelation of the Mystery to Paul and the Apostles (3:2-5)

We in the twenty-first century take it for granted that Gentile Christians are full citizens, but for a Jewish Pharisee in the first century, this would have been considered impossible. That this would be the case was indeed a mystery.

"Surely you have heard about the **administration** of God's grace that was given to me for you, that is, the **mystery** made known to me by revelation...." (3:2-3a)

The obvious keyword in this passage is "mystery." What does it mean? What did it mean to Paul and the recipients of this letter? We see the Greek word *mystērion* in 1:9;

3:3-4, 9; 5:32; and 6:19. "Mystery" in Paul's writings is not a puzzle to be solved by detectives studying the clues, such as in a mystery novel. Among the abundant Greco-Roman mystery religions it meant a secret rite or teaching that only the initiated could know. But Paul uses it quite differently, as "the unmanifested or private counsel of God, (God's) secret," which are hidden from human reason and ingenuity, and can only be known by revelation.[1] Paul is talking about a secret, hidden for the ages and only now ready to be revealed.

Before we get into the text, let's consider another word that is used twice in our passage, *oikonomia*. But its translation can disguise the fact that it is the same word:

Verse 2

- administration (NIV)
- dispensation (KJV)
- stewardship (NRSV)
- commission (NASB)

Verse 9

- administration (NIV)
- fellowship (KJV)
- plan (NRSV)
- administration (NASB)

The basic meaning of *oikonomia* is "responsibility of management, management of a household, work of an estate manager," then more generally, "direction, office." Paul applies the idea of administration to the office of an apostle, "You have heard about the administration of grace that was given to me for you...." (3:2, NIV) The word meaning begins with the planning, administrative process, but then moves to the plan itself. It can mean, "the state of being arranged, arrangement, order, plan," and in this sense is used in 3:9, "the plan of the mystery hidden for ages...." (NRSV).[2]

Now let's look at the passage again:

"[2]Surely you have heard about the **administration** of God's grace that was given to me for you, [3]that is, the **mystery** made known to me by revelation, as I have already written briefly. [4]In reading this, then, you will be able to understand my insight[3] into the **mys-**

---

[1] *Mystērion*, BDAG 661-662.

[2] *Oikonomia*, BDAG 697-698.

[3] "Insight" (NIV), "knowledge" (KJV), and "understanding" (NRSV) is the Greek noun *synesis*, "the faculty of comprehension, intelligence, acuteness, shrewdness" (BDAG 970).

tery of Christ, [5]which was not made known[4] to men in other generations as it has now been revealed by the Spirit to God's holy apostles and prophets." (3:2-5)

Paul tells us that he has been particularly chosen for this mission of revealing God's hidden secret. He makes it a point that it isn't his idea or his discovery or something he figured out, but that "the mystery was made known to me by revelation[5]" (3:3), that is, that God revealed it to him.

Revelation to Apostles and Prophets

The *means* of this revelation is "by the Spirit" (1 Corinthians 2:9-16). The direct *recipients* of this revelation are God's "holy apostles and prophets" (3:5).

Christianity is not a religion that men figured out or inferred. It comes to us by revelation, that is, God revealed it directly to us through inspired writers of Scripture – "holy apostles and prophets."

The Gospels are Jesus' words and actions conveyed to us by apostolic teaching – that is, from the message and with the authority of Christ's appointed apostles.[6] The Old Testament is Scripture because it is a revelation of God through his prophets. The New Testament epistles are Scripture because they are the teaching of the apostles, who were given by Christ the specific task of establishing the church. Scripture is a product of the Holy Spirit's revelation through apostles and prophets. Paul wrote to Timothy:

> "... From infancy you have known the **holy Scriptures**, which are able to make you wise for salvation through faith in Christ Jesus. All **Scripture** is **God-breathed** (*theopneustos*[7]) and is useful for teaching, rebuking, correcting and training in righteousness, so that the man of God may be thoroughly equipped for every good work." (2 Timothy 3:16-17)

This quality of being "God-breathed" (NIV), "inspired" (NRSV, NASB), or "given by inspiration" (KJV) is what makes Scripture authoritative for us in all matters of faith and practice. The sacred teachings of the "holy prophets and apostles" should inform our traditions rather than be subject to our traditions. Where our traditions are in conflict with the spirit and teaching of the Word – as has been the case many times in history – then our traditions need to change, not the other way around. We are an apostolic

---

[4] "Made known" in verses 5 and 10 is the verb *gnōrizō*, "to cause information to become known, make known, reveal" (BDAG 203).

[5] "Revelation" is the noun *apokalypsis*, "making fully known, revelation, disclosure" (BDAG 112).

[6] Mark's Gospel is based on Peter's preaching, according to Irenaeus (c. 175 AD). Luke based his Gospel largely on the same record that Mark used, supplemented by reports from other eyewitnesses (Luke 1:1-4). Matthew and John have long been held to been recorded by these apostles themselves.

[7] *Theopneustos* is a compound word from *theos*, God + *pneō*, to blow, breathe. The word means "inspired by God, God-breathed" (BDAG 449-450; E. Schweizer, *pneuma, ktl.*, TDNT 6:389-455).

church only when we follow the teachings of Christ as given through his appointed apostles without dilution or compromise.

Having said that, Paul's epistles clearly teach us to expect and honor the gift of prophecy (1 Corinthians 11:5; 12:11; 13:2; 14:1-33; 1 Thessalonians 5:20; 1 Timothy 4:14;) and the ministry prophets – those whose primary spiritual gift is prophecy (1 Corinthians 12:29; Acts 11:27; 13:1; 15:32; 21:9-10; Romans 12:6). In Ephesians 4:11 Paul sees the ministry of prophet as a key one in the church. The post-apostolic church also recognized the gift and ministry of prophet.[8]

As much as we are to honor the gift of prophecy, however, the accredited teaching of Christ and his apostles as given in the New Testament Scriptures is our authority and the standard to which any other revelation or prophecy – real or supposed – is to be measured and judged.

Q1. (Ephesians 3:2-5) Why is God's revelation to "his holy apostles and prophets" our authority for faith and practice? What is the danger of minimizing or straying from that revelation? What is the danger of superseding that revelation? What is the danger of denying that God reveals himself to us and to his church today?
http://www.joyfulheart.com/forums/index.php?showtopic=519

What Is the Mystery? (3:6)

Okay, but what is this mystery Paul is talking about?

"This mystery is that through the gospel the Gentiles are heirs together with Israel, members together of one body, and sharers together in the promise in Christ Jesus." (3:6)

That's it! Gentiles are equally the people of God with God's chosen people, the Jews. That may not be a revelation to you, but it sure was an eye-opener to the early Jewish believers – and to the Gentile believers, who were sometimes made to feel like second-class citizens around Jewish Christians.

The Gentiles are described in relationship to Israel with three compound words, starting with the preposition *syn-*, "together with."

---

[8] *Didache* 10.7; 11:3, 7-12. For more on the gift of prophecy, see my articles on "Understanding the Gift of Prophecy" (www.joyfulheart.com/scholar).

1. **"Heirs together"** (*sygklēronomos*), "inheriting together with, co-heir."[9] See also Hebrews 11:9; 1 Peter 3:7; and Romans 8:17.
2. **"Members together of one body"** (*syssōmos*), "belonging to the same body,"[10] used only here in the New Testament.
3. **"Sharers together"** (*symmetoxos*), "having a share with another in some possession or relationship, sharing with,"[11] here and in 5:7.

But lest we Gentiles get big-headed, in Romans Paul makes the point in Romans 9-11 that we are not to look with enmity on the Jews, even the unbelieving Jews.

> "I do not want you to be ignorant of this mystery, brothers, so that you may not be conceited: Israel has experienced a hardening in part until the full number of the Gentiles has come in. And so all Israel will be saved..." (Romans 10:25-26a).

Anti-Semitism is evil – and dangerous – since unbelieving Jews "are loved on account of the patriarchs" (Romans 11:28). If we despise and persecute unbelieving Jews *who are loved by God,* we make ourselves enemies of God's purposes.

Q2. (Ephesians 3:6) Just what is the "mystery" that Paul is talking about? Why was it important to the Gentile Christians in Paul's day?
http://www.joyfulheart.com/forums/index.php?showtopic=520

The Apostolic Servant of This Gospel (3:7-9)

Now Paul talks about the immense sense of privilege that he feels as the primary conveyor of this mystery:

> "7I became a servant of this gospel by the gift of God's grace given me through the working of his power. 8Although I am less than the least of all God's people, this grace was given me: to preach to the Gentiles the unsearchable riches of Christ, 9and to make plain to everyone the administration of this mystery, which for ages past was kept hidden in God, who created all things." (3:7-9)

Paul, as you know, was not one of the original twelve apostles. Rather, he was an arch enemy of the fledgling church, hunting down Christians so they might be tried and put to death for apostasy to Judaism. It was on just such a "search and destroy"

---

[9] *Sygklēronomos*, BDAG 952.
[10] *Syssōmos*, BDAG 978.
[11] *Symmetoxos*, BDAG 958.

expedition that Christ appeared to Paul and gave him a particular commission to the Gentiles:

> "I have appeared to you to appoint you as a servant and as a witness of what you have seen of me and what I will show you. I will rescue you from your own people and from the Gentiles. I am sending you to them to open their eyes and turn them from darkness to light, and from the power of Satan to God, so that they may receive forgiveness of sins and **a place among those** who are sanctified by faith in me." (Acts 26:16b-18; see also 9:15)

That "place among those" is the mystery that God would gradually make known to Paul, that *Gentile believers had every bit as much a place among God's saints as did Jewish believers.*

Though Jesus personally appointed Paul to be an apostle (1 Timothy 2:7; 2 Timothy 1:11; Romans 1:1; 1 Corinthians 1:1; Ephesians 1:1; etc.), he is humbled that he would be chosen. Notice how he describes his ministry:

- **"Servant"** is the Greek noun *diakanos* (from which we get our English word "deacon"), "agent, courier, one who serves as an intermediary in a transaction."[12] A servant only has the power of the one whom he serves, not because of anything in himself.
- **"Gift"** is the Greek noun *dōrea*, "gift, bounty, that which is given or transferred freely by one person to another," carrying the idea of "without payment, gratis."[13] Ministry is a gift, not something we earn or deserve. It is not an office to lord over others, but a gift to them from God.
- **"Less than the least"** is the Greek adjective *elachistos*, a comparative word, "pertaining to being the lowest in status, least."[14] Paul is quite conscious that he had "persecuted of the Church of God" (1 Corinthians 15:9), "a blasphemer and a persecutor and a violent man" (1 Timothy 1:13). He told Timothy, "Christ Jesus came into the world to save sinners – of whom I am the worst" (1 Timothy 1:15). Of anybody, he is the last to deserve such an honor. He never forgot who he had been, but he did not wallow in it, but humbly accepted his task and moved on to God's will for his life.
- **"Preach"** is the verb *euangelizō*, literally, "bring good news, announce good news." Here probably, "proclaim the divine message of salvation, proclaim the

[12] *Diakanos*, BDAG 230-231.
[13] *Dōrea*, BDAG 266.
[14] *Elachistos*, BDAG 314.

gospel, preach."[15] Paul is a bringer-of-Good-News whether that news is accepted or not.

Q3. (Ephesians 3:7-9) Why is Paul so careful to be humble about his call and apostleship? How can his example help us remain as humble servants?
http://www.joyfulheart.com/forums/index.php?showtopic=521

The Unsearchable Riches of Christ (Ephesians 3:8)

Meditate for a moment on the phrase "the unsearchable riches of Christ" (verse 8).

"Unsearchable" (NIV, KJV) or "boundless" (NRSV) is the adjective *anexichniastos*, a compound word from *a-*, "not" + *exichniazō*, "to track out," literally, "not to be tracked out." The meaning here is "inscrutable, incomprehensible, fathomless" (also Romans 11:33).[16] We can't figure God out with our minds and our logical deduction. That's why sometimes theology can become merely speculation, the farther it gets away from what the Scripture reveals. The Scripture just doesn't tell us everything we wonder about, and we need to be careful not to speak dogmatically where the Scripture does not clearly teach something.

Christ's revelation is beyond what we can understand, but it is also rich. **"Riches"** is the noun *ploutos*, with the basic meaning, "abundance of many earthly goods, wealth." Applied to Christ it means "a wealth, abundance."[17] On Christ's riches see also 3:16; 1:7; 2:7; Romans 11:33; Philippians 4:19; Colossians 1:17; 2:2-3. If we have no concept of Christ's riches, we don't desire them *or* him. But Paul had caught a glimpse of a different kind of riches than worldly wealth, was captured by it, and bids us come to explore Christ's riches for ourselves.

The Church Is to Make It Known (3:10-11)

Now Paul comes to the Church's place in all this:

---

[15] *Euangelizō*, BDAG 402.
[16] *Anexichniasto*, BDAG 77.
[17] *Ploutos*, BDAG 832.

"His intent was that now, through the church, the manifold[18] wisdom of God should be made known to the rulers and authorities in the heavenly realms, according to his eternal purpose which he accomplished in Christ Jesus our Lord." (3:10-11)

The church is the agent of making known God's wisdom.[19] But our audience in declaring the Gospel is not only humans who are lost. But it is also the evil spiritual powers[20] that have usurped God's authority here on earth. Just why it is important that we proclaim the Good News in their hearing, we don't really know. But Paul is clearly saying that the Church's proclamation of the Gospel is not merely local and temporal, but cosmic in its importance.

Approaching God through Faith (3:12-13)

Paul has been assuring the Gentile Christians of their full status and full citizenship in the Kingdom of God. On the basis of that status, he encourages them to draw near to God:

"In him and through faith in him we may approach God with freedom and confidence. I ask you, therefore, not to be discouraged because of my sufferings for you, which are your glory." (3:12-13)

Verse 12 contains three Greek words which describe the freedom and wonder of our relationship with the Almighty God through faith:

1. **"Access"** (*prosagōgē*), means "a way of approach, access to someone,"[21] which we discussed in 2:18. We "commoners" have access to come before the King of the Universe with our petitions and our hearts of praise. Remarkable!

2. **"Boldness"** (*parrēsia*) refers to "a state of boldness and confidence, courage, confidence, boldness, fearlessness, especially in the presence of persons of high rank."[22] We are not to be timid before God.

3. **"Confidence"** (*pepoithēsis*) describes "a state of certainty about something to the extent of placing reliance on, trust, confidence."[23] We can be confident of his fa-

---

[18] "Manifold" (NIV, KJV) is *polypoikilos*, "pertaining to being diversified, (very) many-sided."[BDAG 847] It has the idea of "many-faceted." NRSV translates it as the wisdom of God "in its rich variety."

[19] Paul uses the preposition *dia*, a marker of instrumentality or circumstance whereby something is accomplished or effected, "by, via, through" (BDAG 224).

[20] These "rulers and authorities" (NIV, NRSV; "principalities and powers," KJV) are apparently spiritual enemies of God in spiritual realms, perhaps classes of fallen angels. See also 1:21; Romans 8:38; Colossians 1:16; 1 Peter 3:22.

[21] *Prosagōgē*, BDAG 876.

[22] *Parrēsia*, BDAG 781.

vor and love. He delights in us. Like a father who enjoys his children, your Heavenly Father delights in you and longs to spend more time with you.

The writer of Hebrews expresses this glorious access to God:

"For we do not have a high priest who is unable to sympathize with our weaknesses, but we have one who has been tempted in every way, just as we are – yet was without sin. Let us then approach the throne of grace with confidence, so that we may receive mercy and find grace to help us in our time of need." (Hebrews 4:15-16)

Q4. What does Ephesians 3:12 teach us about the manner of approaching God? What happens if we try to pray without these qualities?
http://www.joyfulheart.com/forums/index.php?showtopic=522

Paul the persecutor was surprised by the grace of God. Gentile Christians are surprised to find that it's been God's plan all along to include them as full citizens in the Kingdom of God. And you and I are are surprised – again and again – by the mercy and love of God. Perhaps the words that express our emotions best are "delight" and "joy" in God. But the most surprising thing of all is to realize that our delight and joy in God are a mirror of his love and joy in us, expressed by one of his holy prophets thousands of years ago:

"The LORD thy God in the midst of thee is mighty;
he will save, he will rejoice over thee with joy;
he will rest in his love,
he will joy over thee with singing." (Zephaniah 3:17, KJV)

Thank you, Lord, for your love.

Prayer

Yes, Lord, we give you thanks for your amazing grace and the incredible access we have to you through Jesus and your Spirit. Give us the wisdom to enjoy You so much in this life that we are longing for the next. In Jesus' name, we pray. Amen.

Key Verses

"In him and through faith in him we may approach God with freedom and confidence." (Ephesians 3:12)

---

[23] *Pepoithēsis*, BDAG 796.

8. Paul's Prayer and Doxology (3:14-21)

Paul concludes the first part of his Letter with another prayer for the Ephesians and a doxology of praise to God. It doesn't do justice to this prayer to oversimplify it. However, before we delve into the details, it may help to see the bare bones of Paul's prayer. Note that Paul's Greek is somewhat confusing, so different scholars may construe it a bit differently.[1] But it seems to ask God for two major outcomes:

(a) For inner strengthening by the Spirit (3:16)

Catacomb in of Via Anapo, Rome. Orans or orante fresco, early Christian, mid-third century. This posture of arms lifted in prayer is found in thousands of figures in the catacombs.

(b) **that is**, Christ dwells in your hearts through faith (3:17a)

(c) **that is**, you have been rooted and grounded in love (3:17b)

so that (*hina*)

1. you might comprehend fully the extent of God's mind-blowing love and

2. you might be filled with the fullness of God.

Now let's meditate on some of the details of Paul's prayer.

Kneeling before the Father (3:14-15)

"For this reason I kneel before the Father, from whom his whole family in heaven and on earth derives its name." (3:14-15)

Paul begins this prayer with the words, "for this reason" (*charin*) since he is referring back to the Gentile Christians' destiny to reveal God's plan to spiritual beings in

---

[1] I myself construed this prayer a bit differently in a chapter of *Great Prayers of the Bible*. Paul isn't speaking in precise grammatical and logical propositions, but pouring out an effusive prayer to God followed by a praise.

heavenly places. Paul probably mentions his kneeling posture to emphasize his earnestness in this prayer (also Acts 20:36; 21:5).

God's Resources (3:16)

Now he shares the content of his prayer.

"I pray that out of his glorious riches he may strengthen you with power through his Spirit in your inner being...." (3:16)

Notice the basis of Paul's confidence in God's ability to answer prayer abundantly – God's "glorious riches" – fabulous wealth, unfathomable resources, unimaginable riches and the power they create. You can see this theme in several of Paul's letters (Ephesians 1:7,18; 2:7; 3:8; Romans 9:23; Philippians 4:19; Colossians 1:27). So often we pray out of our own lack of faith, out of our own spiritual poverty. Rather, we must learn to pray based on our belief in God's inexhaustible supply. When we can see that in our mind's eye, our faith can rise to the occasion without hindrance of worrying about how God will ever be able to answer our prayer.

Strengthening the Inner Being (3:16b-17a)

To that end of strengthening our faith, Paul prays that God will "strengthen you with power through his Spirit in your inner being." He uses two "power words" in this verse. The verb "strengthen," *krataioō*, "become strong,"[2] is used right next to the noun *dynamis*, "power, might, strength, force, capability."[3] Together the words have the effect of accentuating the degree of strength and power, "become mightily empowered."[4]

The *means* by which this spiritual empowerment comes about is "though (*dia*) his Spirit." The location of this strengthening is the "inner being" (NIV, NRSV) or "inner man" (KJV). Prior to salvation, our human spirit is spiritually dead, cut off from God. When the new birth occurs, the Holy Spirit is somehow fused with our human spirit making us alive to God, vitally connected to Him through the Spirit, and infused with life of an eternal quality and magnitude (see Romans 8:1-11).

Look at the passage again:

---

[2] *Krataioō*, BDAG 564.
[3] *Dynamis*, BDAG 262.
[4] Literal rendering in *The New Greek-English Interlinear New Testament,* by Robert K. Brown and Philip W. Comfort.

"I pray that out of his glorious riches he may strengthen you with power through his Spirit in your inner being,[5] so that Christ may dwell in your hearts through faith." (3:16b-17a)

Paul now prays a parallel, explanatory statement – "that Christ may dwell in your hearts through faith" (3:17a). Heart (*kardia*, from which we get our word "cardiac") is commonly used in the New Testament to refer to the "center and source of the whole inner life, with its thinking, feeling, and volition."[6] The word "dwell," *katoikeō*, "live, dwell, reside, settle (down),"[7] refers "permanent habitation as opposed to sojourning, pitching a tent or an occasional visit."[8] The Spirit's inner strengthening is the same thing as Christ dwelling in their hearts; these are two ways to express the same truth.[9]

Q1. (Ephesians 3:16-17) Do the concepts of (a) strengthened by the Spirit in the inner person, and (b) Christ dwelling in our hearts say the same thing, or are they separate and distinct ideas? What do you think?
http://www.joyfulheart.com/forums/index.php?showtopic=523

The Process of Sanctification

Does this mean that Paul is praying for the salvation of the Ephesian saints? No. He is assured of their salvation (Ephesians 1:15). I think he is praying that the Spirit might permeate their whole being, through and through. It is possible to be a "carnal Christian" (KJV, 1 Corinthians 3:1) and still be a genuine Christian. But the Spirit has a long way to go to form Christ in your character and train you to follow him. Paul is praying for more, that the work of Christ in us might continue and deepen and grow.

Robert Boyd Munger wrote a short booklet entitled *My Heart, Christ's Home* (1951) that has been widely reprinted. In it he compares the heart to a home. When Christ comes into the heart he is invited into the living room as an honored guest and asked to be seated and to feel right at home. But when Christ starts poking into closets and other

---

[5] The phrase consists of two words: *anthropos*, the generic noun for man, mankind, humankind, with no reflection of male gender, and the adverb of place *esō*, "inside, within." (BDAG 398). See similar expressions in Romans 7:22 and 2 Corinthians 4:16, and the idea expressed in Jeremiah 31:33; Romans 2:29; and 1 Peter 3:4.

[6] *Kardia*, BDAG 508-509.

[7] *Katoikeō*, BDAG 534.

[8] Barth, p. 370.

[9] So Bruce, pp. 326-327; Foulkes, p. 111; Barth, pp. 369-370.

rooms in the house, it is obvious that the host isn't prepared for him. These rooms are off-limits to the influence of Christianity. But you asked me to live here, didn't you? asks Christ.

All of us have sins and selfishness hidden even to ourselves. As Christ's Spirit permeates our entire being, we gradually become more and more surrendered to him, every closet and room, every drawer and chest – and we become more and more filled with a knowledge of him, that is, we come to know him better and better.

Theologically this is called "sanctification." It is a process. Paul is praying here that the process might be accelerated in the Ephesian believers. For without sanctification, our view of God and our faith is so diminished and straitjacketed that we can hardly see God in his fullness (Hebrews 12:14), nor can we be truly filled with the Spirit.

Spirit-filled Christians

Certain groups of Christians refer to themselves as "Spirit-filled." By this they mean, perhaps, that they have had a Pentecostal experience. Praise God for a Pentecost-like experience of the God of the supernatural! I know first-hand how wonderful and faith-expanding that can be. But, dear friends, "Spirit-filled" is a deceptive and somewhat prideful jargon phrase. By definition all Christians *have* the Spirit (Romans 8:9b). Remaining *filled* with the Spirit requires a day-by-day surrender to God, a dealing with and giving up of sins that he reveals, and being stretched by God to open more to receive more of his infinite Being. Dear friends, may we all be truly "Spirit-filled," not as a mark of distinction from lesser Christians, but as a description of the Spirit's gracious and present work in our lives. To be Spirit-filled is to be humbled, not proud.

Rooted and Grounded in Love (3:17b)

Paul has described a Christian's relationship to God by (1) being empowered by the Spirit in the inner person, by (2) Christ dwelling in our hearts by faith. Now he adds a third, by (3) being rooted and grounded in love.

> "And I pray that you, being rooted and established in love, may have power, together with all the saints, to grasp how wide and long and high and deep is the love of Christ, and to know this love that surpasses knowledge – that you may be filled to the measure of all the fullness of God." (3:17b-18)

Paul refers to their present level of understanding as being rooted (*rizoō*) and grounded (NIV, KJV) or established (NRSV) in love. The second verb is *themelioō*, "to provide a base for some material object or structure, lay a foundation," then figuratively, "to provide a secure basis for the inner life and its resources, establish, strengthen."[10]

Remember that one of Paul's petitions that we're getting to in verses 18-19a is to fully comprehend Christ's love. Paul has recently heard of the Ephesians' "love for all the saints" (1:15b), so they are not without love. But that practice of love must be deepened. He is asking in verse 17b that the Ephesians might be "rooted and grounded in love," that is, that love might more and more be their way of life. Only if we know the experience of loving hard-to-love people, can we truly comprehend the ins and outs of Christ's immense love.

Outcome 1: To Comprehend the Love that Surpasses Knowledge (3:18-19a)

Having prayed for the Ephesians' practice of love, Paul gets to the first outcome he seeks for the Ephesians:

> "And I pray that you ... may have power, together with all the saints, to grasp how wide and long and high and deep is the love of Christ,[11] and to know this love that surpasses knowledge...." (3:17b-19a)

He prays for them "power to grasp," a phrase with two verbs. The first verb (*exischuō*) means, "to be fully capable of doing or experiencing something, be strong enough."[12] The second verb (*katalambanō*) involves the imagery of chasing someone and seizing him, then used figuratively, to "understand, grasp, learn about something through the process of inquiry."[13] This is the power to grasp, the ability to comprehend the incomprehensible. How can Christ love those who are his enemies? How can God send his only begotten Son into a den of serpents to redeem them? To the natural mind it doesn't make sense. It is truly mind-blowing. He acknowledges this with the phrase "love that surpasses knowledge" (3:19a), using the verb *hyperballō* that we saw in Paul's earlier prayer in 1:19, which means, "to attain a degree that extraordinarily exceeds a point on a scale of extent, go beyond, surpass, outdo."[14]

But he doesn't just pray that we might "get it." He prays that we might grasp the *full scope* of his love – width, length, height, and depth. Wow! Have I achieved this? I don't

---

[10] *Themelioō*, BDAG 449.

[11] Is he praying that they are able to understand Christ's *love for them* or that they themselves would be able to *love others*? Both probably. Grammatically, the term "love of Christ" can be taken as either subjective genitive or objective genitive. But no doubt it begins with understanding Christ's love for us and grows from there.

[12] *Exischuō*, BDAG 350.

[13] *Katalambanō*, BDAG 520.

[14] *Hyperballō*, BDAG 1032.

think so. There are many people I have trouble loving, which is an indication of how little I really comprehend the immensity of God's great love. Father, fulfill Paul's prayer in my own heart!

Q2. (3:18-19) What kinds of things prevent us from comprehending the far reaches of Christ's love? What happens in the way we live when we *do* comprehend, know, and experience this love? What would be different about your life if you could grasp this?
http://www.joyfulheart.com/forums/index.php?showtopic=524

Outcome 2: Filled with God (3:19b)

Now we come to the second outcome Paul seeks for the Ephesians:

"... That you may be filled to the measure of all the fullness of God." (3:19b)

He doesn't want the believers to be half-filled, but filled (*plēroō*) completely. The term "fullness" (*plērōma*), which we saw in 1:23 (chapter 2, footnote 13) suggests "sum total, fullness, even (super)abundance."[15] Paul prays for the Ephesian Christians to be filled with "all the fullness of God." Robinson comments: "No prayer that has ever been framed has uttered a bolder request."[16]

What does it mean to be "filled with all the fullness of God"? Going back to Munger's analogy of Christ having access to all the "rooms" in our "house," it means unlocking some doors and cabinets that have been hitherto closed to Christ's influence – and cleaning them out. Each of us has suffered wounds. In many of us, these hurts have not healed, but underneath the scab are festering sores of bitterness. If that is the case, we must go back, open up the wound, dress it with forgiveness, and cover it this time with God's grace that can cover a multitude of sins. Unlocking some of those doors may require rethinking our value system that has been too strongly influenced by the culture and realigning it with the Word of God. It may involve a change in the way we treat people. Perhaps making amends and asking forgiveness. Dear friends, if you and I want to be filled with all of the fullness of God, that requires Christ's access to and welcome in

---

[15] *Plērōma*, BDAG 829.

[16] Joseph Armitage Robinson, *St. Paul's Epistle to the Ephesians* (London, 1964), cited by Foulkes, p. 114. In verse 19, Barth renders the phrase, "Filled with all the fullness of God," as "May you become so perfect as to attain to the full perfection of God." (Barth, Comment VI. "Head, Body, and Fullness," *Ephesians* 1:200-210). Barth draws on the research of G. Münderlein, "Die Erwählung durch das Pleroma – Bemerkungen zu Kol. 1, 19," *New Testament Studies* 8 (1962), 264-276. Barth also comments on the meaning of *plērōma* in *Ephesians* 1:367, 374.

every area of our lives, no matter how much pain his entrance might entail. He must have all of us if he is to fill us completely.

Years ago, Dr. Sam Shoemaker advised people, "Give all you know of yourself to all you know of God." That requires our increased knowledge to be matched by a renewed dedication to God. To engage in Bible study to expand the mental understanding without a commensurate willingness to surrender our lives to conform to that knowledge is both hypocritical and dangerous (James 3:1). Bible study requires engaging both mind and heart in a dual quest to know God more fully and be possessed by him more completely.

What a profound prayer Paul prays for the Ephesians – and for us – "...that you may be filled to the measure of all the fullness of God." (3:19b)

Q3. (Ephesians 3:16, 19) What does it mean to be "filled with the Spirit" (verse 16)? Is this a one-time experience or a continual reality? What can we do to be filled with the Spirit? Is it different or the same as being "filled with all the fullness of God" (verse 19)?
http://www.joyfulheart.com/forums/index.php?showtopic=525

Doxology: God's Ability to Answer Abundantly (3:20)

Now Paul concludes his prayer – and indeed, the first half of Ephesians – with a doxology, literally a "word of glory" (Greek *doxa*, "glory + "*logos*, "word"). "Doxologies are short, spontaneous ascriptions of praise to God,"[17] usually having three parts: (1) the One to whom glory is given, (2) the ascription of "glory," and, in Paul's doxologies, (3) the expression "forever and ever." The New Testament includes other doxologies in Romans 16:25-27; Philippians 4:20; 1 Timothy 1:17; 1 Peter 4:11, 5:11; 2 Peter 3:18; Jude 24-25; and Revelation 1:6, to name a few. Let's examine this one:

> "Now to him who is able to do immeasurably more than all we ask or imagine, according to his power that is at work within us...." (3:20)

Paul uses two words to describe the degree of God's ability to answer prayer:

"Far more" (NRSV), "more" (NIV), and "above" (KJV) translate the first abundance word, *hyper*, "over and above, beyond, more than," "a marker of a degree beyond that of a compared scale of extent, in the sense of excelling, surpassing."[18]

---

[17] Patrick T. O'Brien, "Benediction, Blessing, Doxology, Thanksgiving," DLP, p. 69.
[18] *Hyper*, BDAG 1030-1031,B.

"Exceeding abundantly" (KJV, cf. NRSV) and "immeasurably" (NIV) is *hyperekterissou*, "quite beyond all measure," the highest form of comparison imaginable.[19] This word is also used in 1 Thessalonians 3:10 and 5:13. Barth translates the phrase, "to outdo superabundantly."[20] 234

Notice that the limiting factor is not what we can ask or imagine. The limiting factor is the power (*dunamis*) that is working (*energeō*) in us. Whose power? God's power! Remember in Paul's first prayer for the Ephesians (1:19), the eyes of our hearts were to be opened to "his incomparably great power."

There is no limit to God's power. Our ability to comprehend God's power and desire to bless is surely limited, thus limiting the scope of our prayers. But God's power is infinite, limitless. As song "He Giveth More Grace" says:

> "His love hath no limit,
> His grace hath no measure,
> His power hath no boundary known unto man.
> But out of his infinite riches in Jesus,
> He giveth, and giveth, and giveth again."[21]

Notice that this immeasurable power is "his power that is at work within us" (3:20). Paul glorifies God that this incredible power works in and through[22] us believers. How can we feel so powerless when the unbounded power of God is ready to work through us? The great saints of history could work miracles because their faith was unfettered by the unbelief fostered by a tradition of "excuse-ourselves" theology. Can you see why Paul prays that the "eyes of our hearts" be opened? When the blinders come off, the power can be released.

Doxology: Glory in the Church (3:21)

Having described God's infinite power and capability that exceeds our ability to pray, Paul breaks into full doxology, a full word of glory:

---

[19] *Hyperekterissou*, BDAG 1033.

[20] Barth, p. 375.

[21] "He Giveth More Grace," words: Annie Johnson Flint, music: Hubert Mitchell (© 1941. Renewed 1969 Lillenas Publishing Company).

[22] The Greek preposition *en* here can be either (1) locative – in the location or sphere of our persons, or (2) instrumental – by means of us, or through our agency. In either case the idea is the same. H.E. Dana and Julius R. Mantey, *A Manual Grammar of the Greek New Testament* (Macmillan, 1927, 1955), §112. BDAG 326-330.

"To him be glory in[23] the church and in Christ Jesus throughout all generations, for ever and ever! Amen." (3:21)

In this doxology there are two sources of glory accruing to God: (1) from the church and (2) from Christ Jesus. Of course, God receives glory when Christ is seen. But Paul's deep conviction is that the Church – that is, your congregation and mine, and hundreds of thousands more throughout the world – yes, the Church is to bring glory and credit to God. This is a startling concept, given that the Church has accrued through its history more than its share of black marks and sordid deeds. But it has also seen times of courage and power during persecution and life-giving aid when times were dark. Jesus said, "I will build my Church, and the gates of hell shall not prevail against it" (Matthew 16:18).

In fact, in just the last 50 to 100 years, the Church has brought great glory to God. Think, for example, of the house church movement in China that is transforming a nation. Think of Africa becoming more than half Christian in the twentieth century. Recall South Korea and many other places. When the final story is told and the hidden deeds exposed for all to see, the glory of God *will* be seen in his Church.

Sometimes we see the faults so clearly that we can't see the glory. But we cannot be satisfied with where we are. Does our congregation bring glory and credit to God? Is our worship focused on what pleases us or what pleases him? Are the leaders of the church being exalted or is Christ? Do the good works of the church point to the love of Christ or are they self-serving? We have a long way to go, but our purpose is clear – to bring glory and credit and honor to our God and King. And so we join our voices with Paul's doxology and fervent wish:

"To him be glory in the church and in Christ Jesus throughout all generations, for ever and ever! Amen."

Q4. (Ephesians 3:21) What might be different in your own congregation if bringing glory to God were considered the very most important function of the church? What would be different in your life if bringing God glory was your most important job, bar none?

http://www.joyfulheart.com/forums/index.php?showtopic=526

---

[23] Here again is the possibility of *en* being either locative or instrumental. If you take it as instrumental, "by means of," the question is: How is the church to bring glory to him? By the way we live and love. By the way we preach the greatness of Christ. By our obedience. And most of all, perhaps, by our praise. But you could also understand this phrase in a locative sense: "To him be glory in (the midst of, among) the church," where *en* means "in, on, at, within, among."

Prayer

Father, open our eyes, expand our understanding, help us to comprehend the immensity of both your love and your power. Break us open from our narrow, blindered views of you so that we might see you as you are in all your glory. And whatever changes in us that will require, we offer you both our permission and our humble desire that you might complete your full work in our hearts and lives. In Jesus' name and for his sake, we pray. Amen.

Key Verse

"Now to him who is able to do immeasurably more than all we ask or imagine, according to his power that is at work within us, to him be glory in the church and in Christ Jesus throughout all generations, for ever and ever! Amen." (Ephesians 3:20-21)

9. One Body – Unity and Diversity (4:1-10)

While the first half of Ephesians is has a big-picture, doctrinal orientation, the second half of the letter focuses on practical applications. Paul has worked to develop the theme of unity in Ephesians 1 - 3. Now he explains how that unity can be achieved. The passage we're about to study offers:

- One Purpose
- Three Commands
- Seven Bonds
- Millions of Unique Giftings

Humility and service are at the basis of unity in Christ. Ford Madox Brown (British Pre-Raphaelite painter, (1821-93)," Jesus Washing Peter's Feet" (1865), oil on canvas, Tate Gallery, London.

One Purpose

"Make every effort to keep the unity of the Spirit through the bond of peace." (4:3)

Someone once said, "If you find a perfect church don't join it – otherwise it wouldn't be perfect any longer." Conflict is a fact of life. If you want a harmonious marriage, don't put a man (from Mars) and a woman (from Venus) together. That's a sure recipe for conflict. Instead, put two very mellow people together who are very much the same. It'll be a calm marriage, but they'll probably die early – of boredom.

Whenever you put differences together – in a marriage or in a church – you get conflicts. The purpose here is not to avoid conflict, but to learn how to deal with it so that unity might prevail. Unity is the purpose of this passage and the theme of the entire letter (see the key verse: Ephesians 1:10).

Three Commands (4:1-3)

To bring about this unity, Paul delivers three commands:

1. "Live a life worthy of the calling which you have received" (4:1)

"As a prisoner for the Lord, then, I urge you to live a life worthy of the calling you have received." (4:1)

We've been called to follow Jesus, to be like him. So we are to live our lives in such a way that we bring credit (glory) to him.

I have two big brass belt buckles. The first says, "Praise the Lord." The second says, "Jesus Is Lord." Whenever I wear them I am acutely aware that what I do and say reflects on Jesus. But we don't have to wear belt buckles or T-shirts for our actions to reflect on Jesus. When people know that we are professing Christians they'll be looking at our lives. "Live a life worthy of the calling," admonishes the Apostle. As regards unity, the Master who prayed that we all might be one (John 17:11), expects us to act out that truth in our Christian community. We are called by our Master to be one; let us live a life worthy of that calling.

Verse 1 speaks of the "calling" with which we have been "called." We get our English word "vocation" from Latin *vocatio*, "summons." The Greek word in our passage is *klēsis*, "call, calling, invitation to experience of special privilege and responsibility."[1] Our calling is a general calling to be disciples, followers of Jesus. This is our "vocation" towards God. The way we "walk" (*peripateō*, KJV) or "live a life" (NIV), or "lead a life" (NRSV)[2] must be "worthy" (*axiōs*[3]) of the One who has called us to follow him. Unless we take this seriously, we are just playing at Christianity. (Yes, we fall short at times. Thank God for forgiveness.) But this high calling (Philippians 3:14; KJV) inspires us to our best. And at our best we are to strive for unity with our Christian brothers and sisters.

Q1. (Ephesians 4:1) According to verse 1, what is the standard of our behavior? What is the "calling" to which God has called us?

http://www.joyfulheart.com/forums/index.php?showtopic=532

---

[1] *Klēsis*, BDAG 549.

[2] *Peripateō*, "walk" then figuratively, "to conduct one's life, comport oneself, behave, live as habit of conduct." (BDAG 803).

[3] *Axiōs* here means, "Pertaining to being correspondingly fitting or appropriate, worthy, fit, deserving" (BDAG 93-94).

2. "Be completely humble and gentle; be patient, bearing with one another in love." (4:2)

> "Be completely humble (*tapeinophrosunē*[4]) and gentle (*prautēs*[5]); be patient (*makrothumia*), bearing with (*anechō*) one another in love." (4:2)

Jesus himself established humility and gentleness as virtues. He treated people with gentleness while he healed them with God's power. His humility attracted people. Jesus said:

> "Come to me all you who are weary and burdened," he said, "and I will give you rest. Take my yoke upon you and learn from me, for I am gentle (*praus*) and humble (*tapeinos*) in heart, and you will find rest for your souls" (Matthew 11:28-29).

While we are eager to impress people, he was eager to bless them.

Pride splits churches. People get their toes stepped on, are rubbed the wrong way, don't feel appreciated, and then begin to gossip and complain. To achieve unity we must continually seek humility and gentleness. The desire for power is closely related to pride, and it too infects unwary believers. At the Last Supper the disciples were arguing about which of them would be considered greatest. Jesus told them: "The kings of the Gentiles lord it over them .... But you are not to be like that. Instead, the greatest among you should be like the youngest, and the one who rules like the one who serves" (Luke 22:24-26). To underscore this he took a towel and a basin and began to wash their feet as might a lowly slave (John 13:4-5).

"Be completely humble and gentle," commands Paul (vs. 2a). Without these qualities, unity will escape us.

The next two character traits are just as important: "Be patient, bearing with one another in love" (vs. 2b). The King James translation of "patient" (*makrothumia*[6]) is "long suffering," and that is often what patience entails: suffering long. We are quick to dispense with annoyances, but Paul says that patience with each other is essential to unity. So is "bearing with (*anechō*[7]) one another in love."

---

[4] *Tapeinophrosunē*, "humility, modesty," from *tapeinos*, "pertaining to being unpretentious, humble" (BDAG 989).

[5] *Prautēs*, "the quality of not being overly impressed by a sense of one's self-importance, gentleness, humility, courtesy, considerateness, meekness (in the older favorable sense)." From *praus*, "gentle, humble, considerate, meek" (BDAG 861).

[6] *Makrothumia*, is a compound word from *makro*, "long, large, great" + *thymos*, "passion." The word carries two ideas: (1) the "state of being tranquil while awaiting an outcome, patience, steadfastness, endurance" and (2) the "state of being able to bear up under provocation, forbearance, patience" (BDAG 612-613).

[7] *Anechō*, "to regard with tolerance, endure, bear with, put up with" (BDAG 78).

Have you ever noticed annoying idiosyncrasies in your spouse or your parents or your pastor? Why do they do that?! We want to set them straight and change them. But ingrained habits are difficult to change. We can split and be alone, or we can "bear with each other" and have unity. Yes, God does change people, but we must allow *him* to be the Changer, and give up the notion that this is our role.

Jesus accepted people, loved them, and his love changed them. Of course, love is at the core of Paul's command, too. "Be patient, bearing with one another in love."

Q2. (Ephesians 4:2) Why are patience and humility so important to preserving unity? What happens to the reputation of Jesus Christ when we have right doctrine along with a sense of arrogance towards those who disagree with us? How are we to be both "gentle" and to "fight the good fight of faith"?
http://www.joyfulheart.com/forums/index.php?showtopic=533

3. "Make every effort to keep the unity of the Spirit through the bond of peace" (4:3)

"Make every effort to keep the unity of the Spirit through the bond of peace" (4:3)

Let's look at some of the words in this command.

"Make every effort" (NIV), "endeavoring" (KJV), "being diligent" (NASB) translates Greek *spoudazō*, "hasten, hurry," then "be zealous or eager, take pains, make every effort, be conscientious."[8] This is the same word Paul uses in 2 Timothy 2:15 "Study to show thyself approved unto God." It indicates zealous effort.

"Maintain" (NRSV) or "keep" (KJV, NIV) the unity is more active than our English translations often indicate. The NASB translation "preserve" captures some of the active idea of Greek *tēreō*, a military term: "keep watch over, guard; keep, hold, reserve, preserve."[9] We are charged to actively guard this unity!

The idea of **"bond"** here denotes what keeps together a house, a garment, or different members of the physical body: the wooden beams, the fastenings, or the ligaments.[10] (See also vs. 16).

This is an earnest and solemn command: "Be very zealous to guard and preserve the unity of the Spirit," the ligaments which hold together the Body in peace.

"Oh, I am breaking the unity for the sake of truth," proclaims one zealous follower. But our zeal needs to be focused on guarding unity. "I am breaking the unity for the

---

[8] *Spoudazō*, BDAG 939.
[9] *Tēreō*, BDAG 1002.

sake of pure doctrine," asserts another. But our purity consists of speaking the truth in love (Ephesians 4:15), and

> "Love is patient, love is kind. Love does not envy or boast ... it keeps no record of wrongs. Love does not delight in evil but rejoices with the truth. Love always protects, always trusts, always hopes, always perseveres. Love never fails" (1 Corinthians 13:4-8)

This doesn't mean that preserving unity is at all easy. We need to be faithful to the truth, to guard the teachings delivered to us from the apostles to pass on to the next generation. We need to contend for the faith once delivered to the saints (Jude 3). But we *must* keep the unity of the Spirit, and we *must* do it in love. We *must!* It is a command.

God cause us to repent of our denominational divorces and pride in our own petty righteousness! Forgive us!

Q3. (Ephesians 4:3) How much energy must we expend on Christian unity? What is "the bond of peace"? How do we strike at peace when we are intent on argument and dissension?
http://www.joyfulheart.com/forums/index.php?showtopic=534

Seven Bonds (4:4-5)

> "There is one body and one Spirit – just as you were called to one hope when you were called – one Lord, one faith, one baptism; one God and Father of all, who is over all and through all and in all." (4:4-5)

Seven elements unite us, says Paul:

1. One body
2. One Spirit
3. One hope
4. One Lord
5. One faith
6. One baptism
7. One God and Father

He urges us to look at the things that unite us, rather than the things that divide us. Sometimes we view the early church through rose-colored glasses. Those were the days!

The church was perfect, the saints were wonderful! I just wish I could recreate the New Testament Church! Right. You don't even have to read very carefully to see division:

- In Corinth, one group was touting the preacher Apollos over the Apostle Paul (1 Corinthians 3:4).
- In Galatia, there was conflict between the Christians who wanted to bring along their legalistic Judaism and those who asserted their freedom in Christ (Galatians 3:1-3).
- In Rome, one group preached while Paul was in prison, just to aggravate him (Philippians 1:17).
- In Philippi, Euodia and Syntyche couldn't get along (Philippians 4:2).

The early church didn't lack conflict, but they worked hard – with the apostles' urging – to preserve, guard, and maintain the unity of the Spirit in the bond of peace, focusing on the things they *did* have in common.

One baptism? Don't Christians disagree about baptism? Babies or believers? Sprinkling, pouring, immersion? We *do* disagree, and it is important to study the scriptures and determine carefully what is right. But baptism is to unite us.

> "For we were all baptized by one Spirit into one body – whether Jews or Greeks, slave or free – and we were all given the one Spirit to drink." (1 Corinthians 12:13)

How can we hold our views of baptism higher than the clear command to guard the unity of faith? We must agree to disagree about some things, but continue to hold love as preeminent, and refuse to break fellowship over these things.

Is there a time to break fellowship? Yes. We see this occasionally in the scripture (1 Corinthians 5:1-2; Revelation 2:14-15; etc.). But it is *always* the time to seek unity.

Millions of Unique Giftings (4:7)

> "But to each one of us grace has been given as Christ apportioned it." (4:7)

Once Paul has established the groundwork for the unity of the church, now he goes on to explain the diversity within the body. "But to each one of us grace has been given as Christ apportioned it" (4:7). "Apportioned" (NIV) or "given ... according to the measure" (KJV, NRSV) is comprised of three words, *didōmi*, "give;" *kata*, "according to;"[10] and *metron*, "measure," here "the result of measuring, quantity, number."[11]

---

[10] The preposition *kata* has a variety of meanings. Here it probably refers to "a marker of norm of similarity or homogeneity, according to, in accordance with, in conformity with, according to" (BDAG 511-513, 5).

The spiritual gifts Christ has given cannot be counted. Oh, they can be classified into types and categories. But look at the variety even then. Billy Graham manifestly has the gift of evangelism. In him this gift works through preaching in mass evangelism settings. But the gift of evangelism also worked through Phillip the evangelist who coupled preaching in villages with miracles and personal witness (Acts 8). Are they both valid? Of course. Does Billy's gift have to be like Phillip's? No.

We serve a God who has created categories of trees – oaks, pines, palms – but within these broad categories we see individual species. On our property we have about 800 oak trees in three species: Interior Live Oak (*Quercus wislizenii*), Valley Oak (*Q. lobata*), and Blue Oak (*Q. douglasii*). But when you look carefully, you can see that some of the Live Oaks are probably a cross with the California Black Oak (*Q. kelloggii*) which thrives at a slightly higher elevation. Besides hybridization we have the effects of soil quality and precipitation. Some of our trees grow well on the sandy loam soil. Others struggle to grow in the crevices of granite outcroppings. Some are tall, others are broader, and still others have long branches, which parallel the ground. In the fall, some trees have wonderfully abundant acorn crops, while others will come ripe another year.

Spiritual gifts are no different. God has made human beings wonderfully diverse.

- Factor 1: physical
- Factor 2: temperament
- Factor 3: family environment
- Factor 4: birth order
- Factor 5: artistic ability
- Factor 6: intellectual ability
- Factor 7: language ability
- Factor 8: emotional sensitivity
- Factor 9: spiritual aptitude
- Factor 10: affluence
- Factor 11: opportunities for development
- Factor 12: talents

But spiritual gifts are ... "spiritual," you protest. Talents are "natural." Says who? It is God who has wired us the way we are, and then flooded us with his Spirit. When God is creating, who is to say what is natural and what is spiritual? The result is wonderfully

---

[11] *Metron*, BDAG 644.

unique and enriching and God-given. How many spiritual gifts are there? Five, nine, nineteen, twenty-six? How about billions!

The Victor Dispensing Gifts (4:8-10)

"This is why it says:
    'When he ascended on high,
    he led captives in his train
    and gave gifts to men.'
(What does 'he ascended' mean except that he also descended to the lower, earthly regions? He who descended is the very one who ascended higher than all the heavens, in order to fill the whole universe.)" (4:8-10)

Paul begins his discussion of spiritual gifts in verse 8 by using the figure of a military victory procession where the conquering general leads the prisoners of war through the streets of the capital and distributes gifts to his subjects from the booty. He quotes Psalm 68:18:

"When he ascended on high, he led captives in his train and gave gifts to men."

If we were to carry though the analogy (and Paul doesn't), the conquering general is the victorious Christ, the captives are perhaps the vanquished spirits of the evil one (Colossians 2:15), and the gifts are spiritual empowerment to build up and perfect his Body, the church.

Verses 9 and 10 are a parenthesis that interprets the word "ascended" in the quotation from Psalm 68:19. Paul sees the ascension as the resurrected Christ's ascension into God's presence in glory, as opposed to his descent from heaven onto the earth in human form to redeem humanity.

Q4. (Ephesians 4:7-10) Who gives spiritual gifts? Can our "natural" talents be related to our "spiritual" gifts? How? What is the difference between a natural God-given talent and a spiritual gift?
http://www.joyfulheart.com/forums/index.php?showtopic=535

In the next lesson we'll study five of the gifts which Christ has given to the church, and how they fulfill the purpose of unity. This purpose of the unity of God's people is primary. It is the cause we must strive for. Our goal isn't structural or organizational unity, some kind of world church. Our goal is spiritual: that the Church of Jesus Christ –

in our congregation, between the congregations in our community, and extending to the bodies of congregations throughout the earth – might practice, with love, the unity of Christ's Body that surely exists in heaven and must exist here on earth so that the world might see Christians who love one another. Jesus put it this way to his sometimes proud and fractious disciples:

> "A new command I give you: Love one another. As I have loved you, so you must love one another. By this all men will know that you are my disciples, if you love one another." (John 13:34-35)

Grant this unity based on love, O Lord, in our lives and in our churches.

Prayer

Dear Lord, help me to love my Christian brothers and sisters – the ones I agree with and the ones that see some things differently than I do. Help me to simply love and so reflect you. We ask you to heal the scandal of schism in your Church so that Jesus might be seen in us and that people will know that we are your disciples. In Jesus' mighty name, we pray. Amen.

Key Verses

> "As a prisoner for the Lord, then, I urge you to live a life worthy of the calling you have received." (Ephesians 4:1)

> "Make every effort to keep the unity of the Spirit through the bond of peace." (Ephesians 4:3)

10. Preparation, Ministry, and Maturity (4:11-16)

Our passage speaks about

- The purpose of pastors and leaders: to develop ministry
- The purpose of ministry: to develop maturity
- The purpose of maturity: unity with Christ and his church

What are apostles, prophets, evangelists, pastors, and teachers?

First we need to define some terms:

Defining an Apostle (4:11a)

"Apostle" (Greek *apostolos*) is compounded from two words, *apo*, "off, away" + *stello*, "to send." It designates one who has been sent with a commission and can mean a "delegate, envoy, messenger."[1] In the NT it is used as a technical term to refer to Christ-designated messengers given authority to speak for him and to establish his church.

Paul's call to be an apostle was sudden and decisive. He was struck from his horse and called by Christ. Caravaggio, "The Conversion on the Way to Damascus" (1600), oil on canvas, 230 x 175 cm, Cerasi Chapel, Santa Maria del Popolo, Rome.

The first apostles were the Twelve. "When morning came, he called his disciples to him and chose twelve of them, whom he also designated apostles" (Luke 6:13). Notice the first thing he did after appointing them: "These twelve Jesus sent out (*apostellō*) with the following instructions...." They were to go to the Jews only, to preach the Kingdom is at hand, to heal the sick, to raise the dead, to cleanse the lepers, and to exorcise demons (Matthew 10:5-8). These first apostles were eyewitnesses of the resurrection, as was Matthias, selected to take Judas' place (Acts 1:22-26).

[1] *Apostolos*, BDAG 122.

The apostles were the first teachers (Acts 2:42) and administrators (Acts 6:1-6) of the church, but these responsibilities were soon spread among others. The apostles performed miraculous signs (Acts 2:43; 2 Corinthians 12:12), conveyed the Holy Spirit by the laying on of hands (Acts 8:17-18), and generally established the church both in Jerusalem and as far as Corinth, Macedonia, and Rome. Thomas is said to have gone to Parthia and as far as India establishing churches. *The Didache* seems to recognize the ministry of apostles and prophets in the late first century.[2]

Do apostles exist today? If so, how does one define modern-day apostles? This is hotly debated. If they do exist, they differ some from the original apostles. For example, they are not eyewitnesses to the resurrection (Acts 1:22). I find C. Peter Wagner's working definition helpful:

> "The gift of apostle is the special ability ... which enables them to assume and exercise general leadership over a number of churches with an extraordinary authority in spiritual matters that is spontaneously recognized and appreciated by those churches."[3]

Examples of apostles might be John Wesley, founder of Methodism, in the past, and perhaps Paul (David) Yonggi Cho, pastor of the largest church in the world in Seoul, Korea, and John Wimber, founder of the Vineyard Christian Fellowship. I would guess that Pope John Paul II probably fit this category, too, since his ministry extended far beyond administering the Vatican, He exerted an influential teaching ministry throughout the world. (Note: Apostleship is a gift endowed by the Spirit, not bestowed by churches. I do not expect all present-day apostles to see eye-to-eye with each other on doctrine. Nevertheless, they can still be gifted and empowered by the Spirit to build His Church.)

When I was in college I met an American missionary who worked in the highlands of Mexico. His main role was visiting and teaching in a circuit of about fifty congregations over which he had responsibility. That seems to me an apostolic ministry, akin to the function of St. Paul in Philippi, Galatia, Corinth, and Ephesus and, later, St. John in the Seven Churches of Asia Minor.

---

[2] *Didache* 11.4-9.

[3] C. Peter Wagner, *Your Spiritual Gifts Can Help Your Church Grow* (G/L Regal Books, 1976), p. 208.

Q1. (Ephesians 4:11) If there were apostles today, why kind of function might they have? What needs do our congregations and regional groupings of churches have that an apostle might meet? How might we detect false apostles? (2 Corinthians 11:13; Revelation 2:2)

http://www.joyfulheart.com/forums/index.php?showtopic=536

Defining Prophets (4:11b)

Prophets in the Old Testament seemed to be lone spokesmen for God such as Elijah, Moses, Samuel, and Malachi, often very unpopular for speaking God's word. Jesus and John the Baptist both functioned as prophets. In the early church, however, the prophets seemed be spread among some of the other leadership roles. We read about prophets who came from Jerusalem to Antioch, among them Agabus who prophesied of future events (Acts 11:27-28; 21:10-11). Prophets and teachers gathered in Antioch to worship and fast and seek God's guidance, and out of that gathering came the prophecy: "Set apart for me Barnabas and Saul for the work to which I have called them" – i.e. their missionary journeys (Acts 13:1-3).

There is little other mention of those who held the office of prophet beyond Philip the Evangelist's four unmarried daughters who prophesied (Acts 21:8-9) and Agabus. An early Christian document, *The Didache*, instructs congregations how to relate to itinerant and resident prophets in the last years of the first century.[4]

Paul encouraged all to prophesy (1 Corinthians 14:5), that is, to speak under the anointing of the Holy Spirit the immediate and upbuilding Word of God. I believe this goes beyond anointed preaching to something else entirely.[5] It is one thing to win someone to Christ, it is another to be an Evangelist. It is one thing to teach a lesson, it is another to be a Teacher. In the same way, while many Christians may prophesy occasionally, few of these will have the ministry of being a Prophet.

Defining Evangelists (4:11c)

Next Paul speaks of evangelists. This role isn't spelled out very well in the New Testament, though clearly it has to do with proclaiming the Good News and comes from the Greek word *euangelizo*, to proclaim good news. The noun is used twice, in a technical

[4] *Didache* 11:10-21; 13:1-8.
[5] I have written further on the gift of prophecy (http://www.joyfulheart.com/scholar/).

ministry sense referring to Philip (Acts 21:8), and in a functional sense referring to Timothy (2 Timothy 4:5).

Philip's ministry involved preaching to the Samaritans and winning them to Christ (mass evangelism, Acts 8:4-13) as well as witnessing to and winning the treasurer of Ethiopia, whom he saw riding in a chariot (one-to-one evangelism, Acts 8:26-40).

In the early church evangelists were probably itinerant preachers of the Gospel, perhaps similar to tent-evangelists of our day. In areas of India, Africa, and elsewhere today, evangelists and evangelistic teams will travel to non-Christian villages to share the Gospel with them. While all Christians have an obligation to share Christ where they are, Pete Wagner once estimated that 10% of the people in churches have the gift of evangelism. Oh, that the gift of evangelism would be stirred up in our churches (2 Timothy 1:6; 4:5)! Instead, in some congregations it is shamefully denigrated as proselytism.

Q2. (Ephesians 4:11) How can we stir up the gift of evangelism among members of our congregations? What might be the earmarks of a person with this gift? How can we encourage and stimulate the Spirit-gifted evangelists in our midst?
http://www.joyfulheart.com/forums/index.php?showtopic=537

Defining Pastors (4:11d)

Because of the Greek syntax of vs. 11, some scholars see pastors and teachers to be combined into one ministry of pastor-teacher.[6] More likely they are overlapping roles.[7]

Our word "pastor" (with the related word "pasture") means, literally, "shepherd." In fact, in Spanish, *El Pastor* can refer to either a herder of sheep or a religious leader. A pastor/shepherd (*poimēn*) led the flock, protected it, guided it to places where there was grass to eat and water to drink. He healed the sheep that were hurt, assisted in birth, and with tenderness cared for the flock. This describes pretty well what a resident spiritual leader does for a group or congregation, which is sometimes referred to as a "flock" (Acts 20:28-29; 1 Peter 5:2-3). The larger the church is, the more pastors are needed. In fact, in the largest churches, the so-called "senior pastor" may well not have actual gift of pastor so much as of faith, leadership, teaching, or administration.

[6] Barth, pp. 438-439.
[7] O'Brien, p. 300.

Often the functional pastors in a Christian community are not the official leaders, but adult Sunday school teachers, small group leaders, house church leaders, etc. You can have a pastoral gift of caring for the spiritual needs of a group of people without having received any official title. Recognition is nice, but not necessary to carrying out this important role. God knows, and it is to him that you serve in this gift.

In the New Testament church, the words "elder" (*presbyteros*), pastor (*poimēn*), and bishop or overseer (*episcopos*) are used synonymously. You can observe this by comparing 1 Peter 5:1-4; 1 Timothy 3:1-7; and Titus 1:5-9.

Defining Teachers (4:11e)

The teacher (*didaskalos*) has a role closely related to the pastoral function, but somewhat specialized. The pastor is more a leader of and carer for people, while the teacher grounds people in truth and helps them to understand the implications of truth as it pertains to their everyday lives.

Of course, none of these lines can be drawn with heavy black markers; they often fade into one another. Timothy was a pastor and teacher, told to do the work of an evangelist. Paul was an apostle, but clearly he functioned as a pastor during part of his ministry, as well as a teacher by his letters when there were no people close by he could pastor. He was an evangelist, and you might argue that he was also a prophet. Jesus, too, took on all these roles in his ministry. Let's recognize people's ministries from God, but let's not prevent them from combining roles in order to fit our doctrines. God's giftings often don't follow our rules and man-made position descriptions. Moreover, we may transition from one core ministry to another over our lifetimes.

Q3. (Ephesians 4:11) How could a person have the spiritual gift of pastor or teacher without having an official position in a church? What must a church do if its "senior pastor" doesn't have the spiritual gift of pastor? Who gives these gifts?
http://www.joyfulheart.com/forums/index.php?showtopic=538

Purpose of the Ministry (4:12)

"It was he who gave some to be apostles, some to be prophets, some to be evangelists, and some to be pastors and teachers, to prepare God's people for works of service, so that the body of Christ may be built up...." (4:11-12)

One problem that afflicts modern churches is a strong clergy-laity distinction. Clergy are to do the work of ministry and the laity are to pay their salaries, benefit from the worship they conduct and the sermons which they give, and generally go away encouraged. Wrong!

Look carefully at verse 12 which tells what apostles, prophets, evangelists, pastors, and teachers are to do:

> "for the perfecting of the saints, for the work of the ministry, for the edifying of the body of Christ" (KJV)

Good. Just what we suspected. Pastors are to perfect, work, and edify. But look again. Is that what it is saying? What if you removed the commas from the sentence? Then it reads:

> "to prepare God's people for works of service so that the body of Christ may be built up" (NIV)

This is entirely different. It makes the apostles, prophets, evangelists, pastors, and teachers to be equippers and trainers, rather than the bottom-line ministers.

The word translated "perfecting" (KJV), "prepare" (NIV), "equipment" (RSV), and "equipping" (NASB) is Greek *katartismos*, from *kata*, "towards" + *artios*, "fit, sound, complete." In classical Greek the verb meant "to put in order, restore, furnish, prepare, equip."[8]

The reason we know that the commas in the KJV convey the wrong meaning is that the Greek does not have three parallel clauses each beginning with the word "for." Rather, the phrase "to prepare God's people for (*eis*) works of service" uses the preposition *eis* which indicates the *goal*[9] of this equipping, that is, carrying out works of ministry. The next clause also uses the preposition *eis*, indicating a second goal, "so that the body of Christ may be built up."

Just to clarify the structure here:

Christ gave apostles, prophets, evangelists, pastors, and teachers

In order to (*pros*) prepare and equip God's people (12a)

For (*eis*) works of service (*diakonia*), (12b)
and for (*eis*) building up the body of Christ (12c)

So that we may reach unity in the faith (13a) *and* grow into the full maturity of Christ (13b - 16)

---

[8] Reinier Schippers, "Right, *artios*," NIDNTT 3:349-351; BDAG 526.
[9] *Eis*, BDAG 290, 4.

In other words, the job of pastors, teachers, and other ministers is to equip, prepare, and train the believers so they can learn to function in their own ministries. This is the way that the church will be built up; not by the leaders doing everything themselves, but by the leaders equipping the rest of the people to function in their own ministries. A church in which only the leaders are working to build the church is weak, it is sick. A healthy congregation is one in which the leaders succeed in motivating, training, and deploying the people in a variety of ministries according to the gifts of each member, all of whom bring strength and depth to the ministry of the Body as a whole, and which bring about the maturity of the Body.

We've spent quite a bit of time on this point because this is one of the chief failings of the organized Church. If we can get this right, we'll be well on our way to effectiveness of ministry *and* maturity.

Q4. (Ephesians 4:12) What's wrong with the old model of the minister or pastor being the main worker in the Church? How does it hinder people in the congregation? How does it hurt the community? What is the purpose of pastors and teachers?
http://www.joyfulheart.com/forums/index.php?showtopic=539

The Nature of a Mature Church (4:13-16)

"... ¹³Until we all reach unity in the faith and in the knowledge of the Son of God and become mature, attaining to the whole measure of the fullness of Christ.

¹⁴Then we will no longer be infants, tossed back and forth by the waves, and blown here and there by every wind of teaching and by the cunning and craftiness of men in their deceitful scheming. ¹⁵Instead, speaking the truth in love, we will in all things grow up into him who is the Head, that is, Christ. ¹⁶From him the whole body, joined and held together by every supporting ligament, grows and builds itself up in love, as each part does its work." (4:13-16)

Look at the description of the healthy, mature church:

- Unity in the faith and in the knowledge of Jesus (13a)
- Attaining to the fullness of Christ (13b)
- Speaking the truth in love (15a)
- Growing up into (*eis*) Christ, the Head of the Body (15b)
- An infrastructure of joined and supporting bones, ligaments, and muscles, which can then support (16a)

- Sustained bodily growth (16b)
- Sustained development of increased strength and new infrastructure as needed (16c)
- Each part of the body doing its work (16d)

When this begins to take shape, we and our churches won't be "infants" which are tossed and blown and manipulated (4:14). People won't be deceiving each other with surface level niceties or "tell it like it is" bluntness which blows the other person away. Instead, we'll be "speaking the truth," but also speaking it "with love." Honesty with tenderness and compassion will build Christ's church in a way that won't require it to be dismantled and rebuilt properly.

I'm impressed by the last phrase of this passage: "as each part does its work" (vs. 16d). This brings us back to where we started. The job of the leaders is to equip each part to do its work. Ultimately, each member must commit himself or herself to giving time and energy to the gifts and ministries God has given.

The purpose of all this is found in two places:

vs. 13b "attaining to the whole measure of the fullness of Christ."

and

vs. 15b "we shall in all things grow up into him who is the Head, that is, Christ."

This sounds very much like the overarching theme of the whole letter found in 1:10 "to bring all things in heaven and on earth together under one head, even Christ."

What does this mean in practice?

1. It requires pastors and teachers to concentrate on their primary role of equipping, and to cease doing everyone else's work.
2. It requires members of the congregation to discover their own ministries and begin to practice them effectively ("so that the body of Christ may be built up") and diligently ("as each part does its work")

It requires leaders to lead and church members to follow their leaders into the exciting task of seeing before our eyes the Church of Jesus Christ begin more and more to feel and sound and act and love like Jesus Christ himself in this world. Amen.

Prayer

Jesus, your Church on earth sometimes seems like it has a long way to go. Help us not to give up on it, but to equip your saints for the work of their ministry and see the mission completed through the help of many gifted, consecrated hands. In your holy name, we pray. Amen.

Key Verses

"It was he who gave some to be apostles, some to be prophets, some to be evangelists, and some to be pastors and teachers, to prepare God's people for works of service, so that the body of Christ may be built up...." (Ephesians 4:12-13)

"Instead, speaking the truth in love, we will in all things grow up into him who is the Head, that is, Christ." (Ephesians 4:15)

11. Putting on Clean Clothes (4:17-32)

We may think of the twenty-first century as secular and hard, proclaiming evil as good and deriding good as evil. And it is. In America we've observed a religious and moral decline from which we had been protected by powerful national revivals in the eighteenth and nineteenth centuries. Much of the good and righteousness that those movements had worked into our national character has dissipated now.

Jesus said to the woman taken in adultery, "Neither do I condemn you. Go and sin no more." "Christ and the Woman Taken in Adultery," by Lucas Cranach the Younger (1515-1586), oil on canvas. The Hermitage, St. Petersburg.

But Paul's day was even worse. His era wasn't "post-Christian" but "pre-Christian," and sin abounded in the great cities of the Greco-Roman culture of the day. Paul calls the Christians of Ephesus to take seriously the work of the Holy Spirit in their lives. What follows in 4:17 through 6:9 is a call to righteousness in all areas of life: speech (5:25-32), sexual mores (5:3-7), use of intoxicants (5:18), family relationships (5:21-6:4), and employer-employee relationships (6:9).

Just previous to this passage, Paul painted an exalted picture of the church as Christ's Body which is upbuilding itself in love (4:1-16). Now he spells out some of the implications of being a part of this community of believers. Vs. 17 begins with the word "so" or "therefore," indicating a transition.[1]

---

[1] The word is Greek *oun*, which is "inferential, denoting that what it introduces is the result of or an inference from what precedes, 'so, therefore, consequently, accordingly, then'" (BDAG 736).

Darkness of the Secular Mind (4:17-19)

> "[17]So I tell you this, and insist on it in the Lord, that you must no longer live as the Gentiles do, in the futility of their thinking. [18]They are darkened in their understanding and separated from the life of God because of the ignorance that is in them due to the hardening of their hearts. [19]Having lost all sensitivity, they have given themselves over to sensuality so as to indulge in every kind of impurity, with a continual lust for more." (4:17-19)

Paul analyzes the moral temper of his day. The secular people in the first century are:

Futile in their minds. The Greek word *mataiotēs* means "state of being without use or value, emptiness, futility, purposelessness, transitoriness."[2] Big thoughts and lots to say, but in the end empty, vain, fruitless.

Darkened[3] in their understanding. Recently I watched a documentary about Albert Einstein and other brilliant physicists of the last century. Einstein could see what no one else could see because he was able to question every presupposition afresh. Some of the presuppositions about the nature of physical matter were wrong, or at least inadequate, so without reexamination, he would not have been able to grasp the truth. Unbelievers are darkened in their understanding because they selectively exclude the light about Jesus. They presuppose that Christianity is wrong. They won't hear of it. They reject it. And consequently they are darkened inside.

Separated from God's life. This selective rejection has shut them off from God's life. "Separated" (NIV) or "alienated" is *apallotrioō*, "estrange, alienate."[4] How very tragic! God's life is all around us, pulsing through the creation. But to miss out on the ultimate reality of the universe because of selective deafness is terribly sad.

Ignorant. The unbelievers just don't know about God. They suffer from "ignorance, unawareness, lack of discernment."[5] But it's not as if they've never heard.

Hardened in their hearts. The reason for their ignorance of God, says Paul, is because they have hardened their hearts. The word is *pōrōsis*, "state or condition of complete lack of understanding, dullness, insensibility, obstinacy."[6] Sometimes people complain about God hardening Pharaoh's heart. Pharaoh was doing pretty well hardening his own heart

---

[2] *Mataiotēs*, BDAG 621.

[3] *Skotizō*, "to become dark, be darkened," then "to be/become inwardly darkened" (BDAG 932).

[4] *Apallotrioō*, BDAG 96.

[5] *Agnoia*, generally, "lack of information about something." Specifically, "lack of information that may result in reprehensible conduct, ignorance, unawareness, lack of discernment" (BDAG 13). Our word "agnostic" comes from *agnoia*.

[6] *Pōrōsis*, BDAG 900.

(Exodus 8:15, 19, 32; 9:7, 34), but God gave him over fully to a hardened heart, and hardened it still more (9:12; 10:20, 27; see Romans 1:24, 26, 28).

Given to sexual immorality. The Greek word *aselgeia* is variously translated "sensuality" (NIV, NASB), "licentiousness" (RSV), and "lasciviousness" (KJV). *Aselgeia* refers to "lack of self-constraint which involves one in conduct that violates all bounds of what is socially acceptable, self-abandonment."[7] It is sexual depravity, utterly outrageous behavior, "with a continual lust for more" (NIV). With the constant portrayal of sex outside of marriage in novels, television and films, this kind of sexual behavior has become widely accepted and acceptable. Unfortunately, sexually loose behavior has become part of our young people's courtship rituals.

Paul paints a dark picture of the unbeliever because he wants his readers to clearly see the contrast between darkness and light, between hell-bent behavior and holiness.

Q1. (Ephesians 4:17-19) Using Ephesians 4:17-19 as a basis, how would you describe (in your own words), the secular, non-Christian mindset of our age? Why are we tempted to conform to its values?
http://www.joyfulheart.com/forums/index.php?showtopic=540

Our New, Holy Self (4:20-24)

"[20]You, however, did not come to know Christ that way. [21]Surely you heard of him and were taught in him in accordance with the truth that is in Jesus. [22]You were taught, with regard to your former way of life, to put off your old self, which is being corrupted by its deceitful desires; [23]to be made new in the attitude of your minds; [24]and to put on the new self, created to be like God in true righteousness and holiness." (4:20-24)

This kind of behavior and empty living has nothing to do with Christ, and what you've been taught about him, says Paul. You've been taught to put off the old, corrupt self, and to put on the new holy and righteous self.

Paul uses the analogy of taking off dirty clothing and putting on clean clothing. We see this kind of language elsewhere in his writings, too (Romans 13:12-14; Colossians 3:10, 14). Is it just a matter of taking off something external? No.

---

[7] *Aselgeia*, BDAG 141. "Impurity" (NIV, NRSV) and "uncleanness" is *akatharsia*, literally, "any substance that is filthy or dirty," figuratively, "a state of moral corruption, immorality, vileness, especially of sexual sins" (BDAG 34). "Lust" (NIV) or "greediness" (NRSV) suggests the fervor of this self-abandonment – *pleonexia*, "the state of desiring to have more than one's due, greediness, insatiableness, avarice, covetousness" (BDAG 824).

"Therefore, if anyone is in Christ, he is a **new creation**; the old has gone, the new has come!" (2 Corinthians 5:17)

"Neither circumcision nor uncircumcision means anything; what counts is a **new creation**." (Galatians 6:15)

We don't become Christians by reforming our ways. God works a basic change inside by his Holy Spirit. Jesus called it being "born again" (John 3:1-8).

When I'm hot and sweaty and filthy, nothing feels better than a nice hot shower. I can luxuriate in the steamy shower and I come out smelling clean. But I would be stupid to put back on my dirty underwear and pants. When I'm clean I want to put on clean clothes, it's only natural. This is Paul's point. You've been "created to be like God in true righteousness and holiness" (4:25), so "put on the new self."

One of our chief problems as Christians is that we rush back to what is familiar, what we're used to. It's so easy to look like and act like unbelievers all over again. Don't admire unbelievers, Paul is saying. They live in darkness and emptiness, and have given over their lives to unbridled sexuality. Don't admire and emulate them. Take off that kind of behavior like you would dirty clothing.

That "old self"[8] has been "corrupted by its deceitful desires" (4:22). I hear echoes here of the Garden of Eden, of Eve's and Adam's desire for something tasty and daring, something which will give them a god-like high (Genesis 3). And all it did was to bring them death, first spiritual and then physical. "Each one is tempted when, by his own evil desire, he is dragged away and enticed," writes James (1:14).

The answer to "deceitful desires" is the work that God is doing in us, making you "new in the attitude[9] of your minds" (4:23). He gradually changes our desires, and with that change come new habits and living patterns. We are to cooperate with what God is doing – "put on"[10] (NIV, KJV) or "clothe yourselves" (NRSV) with the new self. We are to refuse to clothe ourselves with the old dirty clothes any longer, but instead, clothe ourselves with the new self.

---

[8] "Old self" (NIV, NRSV) and "old man" (KJV) is two words *palaios*, "old" and *anthrōpos*, "a person of either sex, with focus on participation in the human race, a human being" (BDAG 81-82).

[9] "Attitude" (NIV) or "spirit" (KJV, NRSV) is *pneuma*, "spirit." The word has a number of meanings, including as the Holy Spirit. Here it refers to "a part of the human personality, spirit" ... "spiritual state, state of mind, disposition" (here as well as Galatians 6:1; 1 Peter 3:4; 1 Corinthians 4:21) (BDAG 832-836, 3c).

[10] *Enduō* means first "the act of putting on," specifically clothing. In the middle voice it has a reflexive idea, "clothe oneself, put on, wear." Metaphorically, it is used very often of the taking on of characteristics, virtues, intentions, etc. (BDAG 333-334, 2b). The same word is used of the Holy Spirit, "until ye be endued with power from on high" (Luke 24:49, KJV).

We are to "put on the new self, created to be like God in true righteous and holiness" (vs. 24). You mean we are created[11] to be like God? Yes. That's what the new nature, the new self, is.

Truth, Anger, and Theft (4:25-28)

> "25Therefore each of you must put off falsehood and speak truthfully to his neighbor, for we are all members of one body. 26"In your anger do not sin": Do not let the sun go down while you are still angry, 27and do not give the devil a foothold. 28He who has been stealing must steal no longer, but must work, doing something useful with his own hands, that he may have something to share with those in need." (4:25-28)

We've just seen the big picture, the ideal. Now Paul starts to spell out some of the nitty-gritty implications with another "therefore" in verse 25.

Speaking Truthfully (4:25)

The first change is in our speaking. If God is truth, then we must leave our clever white lies – Paul calls it falsehood – and, instead, speak truthfully. As we discussed in the previous chapter in this study, we don't have to be cruel in our truth-telling. Instead, "speaking the truth in love, we will in all things grow up into him" (4:15). If God is the ultimate truth, and we are "created to be like God" (4:24), then we too must speak like our Father, and put away forever the double-speak of our former father, the father of lies (John 8:44). The reason for speaking truth within the Christian community is plain: "for we are all members of one body" (4:25).

Controlling Anger (4:26-27)

> "'In your anger do not sin': Do not let the sun go down while you are still angry, and do not give the devil a foothold." (Ephesians 4:26-27)

Anger (*orgizō*[12]) is next to shrivel under the awesome light of God's examination. Paul quotes Psalm 4:4, "In your anger do not sin; when you are on your beds, search your hearts and be silent."

Paul recognizes that anger itself is not sin. Anger can be a natural reaction to injustice, the emotion that God gives us so we will not passively allow injustice to have its way forever. But we must be very careful of anger.

---

[11] *Ktizō*, "to bring something into existence, create," used here and in Colossians 3:20 of the new birth (BDAG 572).

[12] *Orgizō* is the verb form of *orgē*, which can have two connotations: (1) "a state of relatively strong displeasure, with focus on the emotional aspect, anger", and (2) "strong indignation directed at wrong-doing, with focus on retribution, wrath" (BDAG 720-721). Our passage reflects the first definition.

1. **Selfishness**. Anger can spring from selfishness as well as injustice. We must observe our motives carefully, so that we don't justify "righteous anger," when it has much more to do with self than with righteousness.

2. **Control**. Anger impels us to overflow our inhibitions and take action. It is a powerful emotion designed to overcome our passivity. But without careful self-control our anger can become abusive, violent, and sinful. "In your anger do not sin," says Paul (4:26). Anger can cause us to say and do things that hurt the people we love and that we regret later.

3. **Bitterness**. Anger can turn into a deep-seated bitterness if we don't deal with it. "Do not let the sun go down while you are still angry," advises the Apostle (4:26b). If we practiced this advice diligently, we would cut the workload of a lot of psychologists and psychiatrists – and pastors, for that matter. A lot of our psychological stresses and abnormalities have resulted from buried anger, rather than anger which was openly dealt with and resolved quickly.

4. **Foothold for Satan**. Anger can "give the devil a foothold" (4:27). We know how that works. When we're angry, our inhibitions are less, and many times we speak our mind without the normal barriers which keep a civil tongue in our mouth. Once we've said some of those angry, nasty, bitter, hurtful things, we can't recall them.

For a long time I wasn't really aware when I was becoming angry. I had decided that I wasn't angry. Period. But refusing to recognize the symptoms of anger kept me from the protection I needed from seeing the warning signs and being careful. It's way too easy to "give the devil a foothold" when we don't own up to our anger, and begin to control it. Anger itself isn't sin, but if not checked, it soon results in sin.

> "A fool gives full vent to his anger,
> but a wise man keeps himself under control." (Proverbs 29:11)

> "Like a city whose walls are broken down
> is a man who lacks self-control." (Proverbs 25:28)

God is known throughout the Bible as "slow to anger" (Exodus 34:6). We need to stop making excuses for our temper tantrums and become like our Father.

Q2. (Ephesians 4:26-27). Why did God give us the emotion of anger, do you think? How can anger be dangerous? How can we keep from sinning when we are angry? Is anger itself sin?

http://www.joyfulheart.com/forums/index.php?showtopic=541

Theft (4:28)

> "He who has been stealing must steal no longer, but must work, doing something useful with his own hands, that he may have something to share with those in need." (Ephesians 4:28)

For the Christian, stealing,[13] too, must go. Many people today are used to taking things so long as they think they can get away with it. Shoplifting is rampant. People steal pencils and supplies from their offices, copies from the company copy machine, and time from their workday – and think nothing of it. When the boss is watching we are scrupulous, but when he is elsewhere, we steal with impunity. Our culture is beginning to smirk at dishonesty as something smart. Getting away with it is mark of our cleverness.

But God's Holy Spirit doesn't let us get away with this for long. First, Jesus reminds us to treat others as we, ourselves, would like to be treated. Stealing isn't wrong just because it defrauds someone else. It is wrong because it avoids "work, doing something useful with his own hands" (4:28b). Work is not a necessary evil, it is good. God worked for six days and rested on the seventh. Jesus supported his family as a carpenter until being about his Father's work captured his full-time attention. We may look down on people who are taking advantage of the welfare system, but if we steal, we are no better.

A third reason for not stealing is that stealing is the opposite of giving. A person who is a "taker" is seldom a "giver," and our God is the ultimate Giver. The former thief is admonished to do honest work "that he may have something to share with those in need" (4:28c).

Blithering, Blathering, Bitterness, and Brawling (4:29-32)

> "[29]Do not let any unwholesome talk come out of your mouths, but only what is helpful for building others up according to their needs, that it may benefit those who listen. [30]And do not grieve the Holy Spirit of God, with whom you were sealed for the day of redemption. [31]Get rid of all bitterness, rage and anger, brawling and slander, along with every form of malice. [32]Be kind and compassionate to one another, forgiving each other, just as in Christ God forgave you." (4:29-32)

It is interesting to note how much of the "new self" has to do with our altered speech patterns. James, of course, talks a good deal about the evil done by the tongue (James 3:1-12). "If anyone considers himself religious and yet does not keep a tight reign on his tongue, he deceives himself and his religion is worthless" (James 1:26).

---

[13] Stealing is the Greek verb *kleptō*, from which we get our English word "kleptomaniac."

Ephesians 4:29 contains a lot of truth in a few words. "Do not let any unwholesome talk come out of your mouths," he says first. The word "unwholesome" (NIV, NASB), "evil" (NRSV), "corrupt" (KJV), is Greek *sapros*. The basic meaning is "spoiled, rotten," used literally of spoiled fish, decayed trees, rotten fruits, and stones that are unsound or crumbling. Figuratively, it means "bad, evil, unwholesome to the extent of being harmful."[14]

Just what *is* coming out of our mouths? In the latter part of verse 29, Paul gives three guidelines for judging our words:

1. **Is it helpful for building others up?** Does it edify? Does it enlighten? Does it encourage?
2. **Is it according to the hearer's needs?** Or only *our* need to vent our frustrations? Does he really *need* this? Does she really *need* this? Some things need to be said, however hard. But many of the things we say could just as well be left unsaid.
3. **Is it beneficial to the hearer?** If love is our mainstay, then benefiting others is our way of life.

Our speech can destroy or heal, it can rip apart or it can build up. And our words lie at the very heart of our Christian religion, according to James.

Paul identifies in particular, "all bitterness, rage and anger, brawling and slander, along with every form of malice." Slander (*blasphēmia*) is "speech that denigrates or defames, reviling, denigration, disrespect, slander."[15] I've caught myself telling stories about people that were intended to lower them in the eyes of others. Shame! That is slander. Paul is speaking directly to me – and you.

Q3. (Ephesians 4:29-32) What kind of "unwholesome talk" is common among us Christians? What three guidelines does Paul give us to measure the value of what we say? What is slander? How common is it among Christians? How can we prevent it?
http://www.joyfulheart.com/forums/index.php?showtopic=542

[14] *Sapros*, BDAG 913.
[15] *Blasphēmia*, BDAG 178.

Grieving the Holy Spirit of God (4:30)

> "And do not grieve the Holy Spirit of God, with whom you were sealed for the day of redemption." (4:30)

Our words can "grieve the Holy Spirit of God." *Lypeō* means "to cause severe mental or emotional distress, vex, irritate, offend, insult."[16] We are indwelt by the Spirit, but our words can insult the Spirit; we can offend Him by our words. We see this phrase to "grieve the Holy Spirit" in Isaiah:

> "Yet they rebelled
> and grieved[17] his Holy Spirit.
> So he turned and became their enemy
> and he himself fought against them." (Isaiah 63:10)

We may have trained ourselves not to offend minorities with insensitive statements. We may be *politically correct*, but are we zealous to be *spiritually correct*? When we seek to blend in and please unbelievers, we may be offending and grieving our very best Friend. Our words can cause deep pain to others – and to the One who loves us deeply – God himself.

Have you ever met an angry man? An angry woman? They're short with us. They're on a short fuse, and can easily explode into "bitterness, rage and anger, brawling and slander, along with every form of malice" (4:31). Some people brawl with their fists; others brawl with their mouths. Slander is saying degrading things about another person to lessen people's opinion of them. How often we judge people out loud. "I would say it to their face," we may comment, but we seldom do. Instead, we slander them hoping to gain a bit of superiority by so doing.

Christians can't afford to keep their smoldering anger, their bubbling bitterness, for it will destroy them, their testimony, and those around them. What can we do? Confess our anger and bitterness to God and plead with him to take it from us. Repent of our "righteous anger" and call it what it is: sin. While there *is* such a thing as righteous anger, most of the time, "man's anger does not bring about the righteous life that God desires" (James 1:20).

Can God remove our anger? Certainly. He may not remove it overnight, since we didn't develop it overnight. Part of it is a habit and a learned behavior. The Spirit will

---

[16] *Lypeō*, BDAG 604.
[17] *'Asab* refers to both physical pain as well as emotional sorrow, "grieve, displease, vex, wrest" (Ronald B. Allen, *'asab*, TWOT #1666).

help us unlearn it if we will become humble before God and be willing to be humbled. Part of dispensing with inbred anger is gained by practicing what is in the next verse.

Kind, Compassionate, Forgiving (4:32)

The final verse of our passage calls on us to:

> "Be kind[18] and compassionate[19] to one another, forgiving[20] each other, just as in Christ God forgave you." (4:32)

Instead of a self-centered attitude that the world revolves around you, Paul commands kindness and compassion towards each other. We don't return evil for evil, but instead good. And these actions aren't just for someone else's benefit. The real cure for our *own* bitterness and pent-up anger is forgiveness.

Sometimes we withhold forgiveness because we don't think that the person deserves forgiveness. While we are probably correct in our assessment, it shows that we don't understand forgiveness. Forgiveness, like grace, is neither earned nor deserved. It is granted freely, unilaterally, by the giver, with no thought to the worth of the one receiving it. Years ago, as a pastor I found myself explaining again and again what forgiveness was *not*, since it is so commonly misunderstood. Finally I wrote it down in an article, "Don't Pay the Price of Counterfeit Forgiveness,"[21] where forgiveness is explained more fully. Paul reminds us that we are to forgive "just as in Christ God forgave you" (4:32b).

Q4. (Ephesians 4:32) Why is it so difficult to forgive those who hurt us? According to Ephesians 4:32, who is our example of forgiveness? What heart attitudes toward people are evidence of a forgiving spirit, according to verse 32a?
http://www.joyfulheart.com/forums/index.php?showtopic=543

---

[18] *Chrēstos*, here pertains to being morally good and benevolent, "kind, loving, benevolent" (BDAG 1090, 3bα).

[19] *Eusplangchnos*, pertaining to having tender feelings for someone, "tenderhearted, compassionate" (BDAG 413).

[20] *Charizomai*, which appears twice in verse 32, comes from the same root as *charis*, "grace." The main idea is "to give freely as a favor, give graciously." Related to money, it means "to cancel a sum of money that is owed." Here, it denotes, "to show oneself gracious by forgiving wrongdoing, forgive, pardon" (BDAG 1078).

[21] Ralph F. Wilson, "Don't Pay the Price of Counterfeit Forgiveness" (*Moody Monthly*, October 1985, http://www.joyfulheart.com/ maturity/forgive.htm)

The key to putting on the new self, is following Jesus, emulating him, making him our new Role Model. The clever unbelievers were once our role models, but no more. "Put ye on the Lord Jesus Christ," Paul reminds us, "and make not provision for the flesh, to fulfill the lusts thereof" (Romans 13:14, KJV).

We are part of Christ's body, part of the church, a new creation, a new self. We've taken an invigorating shower. Let's make sure we put on clean clothes.

Prayer

Father, we so much want to walk in your cleanness. Forgive us for our sins. Change our ways so that they bless you rather than grieve your Spirit. Help us to put on, as clean clothes, "the new self, created to be like God in true righteousness and holiness." Grant it for us, we pray, in Jesus' name. Amen.

Key Verses

"... Put on the new self, created to be like God in true righteousness and holiness." (Ephesians 4:24)

"'In your anger do not sin': Do not let the sun go down while you are still angry, and do not give the devil a foothold." (Ephesians 4:26-27)

"Be kind and compassionate to one another, forgiving each other, just as in Christ God forgave you." (Ephesians 4:32)

12. Imitate Your Father, Children (5:1-20)

When children are little, they begin to mimic their parents. Little toddlers will put on their father's shoes and make big pretense of taking big steps in them. They play house, play store, play church, play school, play war, and in so doing they begin to learn – by imitation.

This passage in this chapter of our study is a continuation of the previous chapter's discussion of the specific behaviors that Christians are to "put on" like clean clothing, and ungodly behaviors which need to be "taken off."

As the child Jesus imitated his father Joseph, so we are to seek to imitate our Heavenly Father. Gerard (Gerrit) van Honthorst (1590–1656), detail of "The Childhood of Christ" (c. 1620), Hermitage, St. Petersburg.

Imitators of God (5:1-2)

"Be imitators of God, therefore, as dearly loved children and live a life of love, just as Christ loved us and gave himself up for us as a fragrant offering and sacrifice to God." (5:1-2)

What a wonderful picture of learned godliness! The Greek word used here is *mimētēs*, "imitator,"[1] one who uses someone as a model, imitates, emulates, follows, from *mimos*, "an actor, mimic". (See also 1 Corinthians 4:16; 11:1; Hebrews 6:12; 1 Thessalonians 1:6.) This is a common theme in the New Testament.

"Your attitude should be the same as that of Christ Jesus...." (Philippians 2:5)

"To this you were called, because Christ suffered for you, leaving you an example, that you should follow in his steps." (1 Peter 2:21)

Paul's picture in Ephesians is of little children imitating their father. And not just children, but "beloved children" (NRSV), "dearly loved children" (NIV), "dear children" (KJV).

---

[1] *Mimētēs*, BDAG 652. W. Michaelis, *mimeomai, ktl.*, TDNT 4:659-674.

As we follow the Father, we will learn to love as he loves, and begin to "live a life of love, just as Christ loved us...." We will learn to live the kind of life Christ lived when he ministered to people and ultimately gave him up as a "fragrant offering and sacrifice to God." Imitation is another way to look at the learning posture of discipleship – "We love because he first loved us" (1 John 4:19).

Sexual Purity (5:3-7)

"³But among you there must not be even a hint of sexual immorality, or of any kind of impurity, or of greed, because these are improper for God's holy people. ⁴Nor should there be obscenity, foolish talk or coarse joking, which are out of place, but rather thanksgiving. ⁵For of this you can be sure: No immoral, impure or greedy person – such a man is an idolater – has any inheritance in the kingdom of Christ and of God. ⁶Let no one deceive you with empty words, for because of such things God's wrath comes on those who are disobedient. ⁷Therefore do not be partners with them." (5:3-7)

Immorality flourished in the Gentile world. If you've ever read Greek mythology, you've discovered that the morals of the Greek gods left something to be desired. If rape, adultery, lust, and sexual enticement are the stuff of gods, how do you expect mere mortals to act? The urban culture of Paul's day was more blatantly immoral than even America's eroding standards. But Christians were expected to live exemplary lives.

Avoiding Sexual Immorality (5:3)

It's obvious from the history of men and women in the church that sex outside of marriage remains a strong temptation. That is why Paul cautions so clearly and explicitly to bring into check our sexual lives as well as other parts of our lives.

"But among you there must not be even a hint of sexual immorality, or of any kind of impurity, or of greed, because these are improper for God's holy people." (4:3)

The word translated "sexual immorality" here is Greek *porneia*, "unlawful sexual intercourse, prostitution, unchastity, fornication."[2] A *pornē* was a prostitute or harlot, from which we get our word "pornography." The KJV tends to translate *porneia* as "fornication," but this is too narrow. "Fornication" is defined in English as "consensual sexual intercourse between two persons not married to each other."[3] *Porneia*, on the other hand, includes not only fornication, but adultery, homosexuality, and any other kind of imaginable sexual perversion.

---

[2] *Porneia*, BDAG 854. Also Friedrich Hauck and Siegfried Schulz, *pornē, ktl.*, TDNT 6:579-595.
[3] *Merriam-Webster's 11th Collegiate Dictionary.*

Incidentally, the word "prude" (which originally was short for "good woman" or "prudent woman") now means "a person who is excessively or priggishly attentive to propriety or decorum; especially a woman who shows or affects extreme modesty."[4]

I once had a couple in my church who became fond of each other and then became engaged to be married. Both of them loved the Lord. Both were children of the '60s. The man had grown up in the California surfer culture and sex between two people who loved one another seemed right to him. She wasn't so sure. I patiently explained what the scripture taught from Old Testament to New, but he couldn't see it. His culture had blinded him. However, he said, "Pastor, though I don't see anything in the Bible against sex before marriage, I'll abstain because you say so." His bride looked relieved. And eventually they were married, and enjoy, I am sure, the joys of marriage together.

Paul is even more specific in 1 Thessalonians as he instructed a pagan culture in ways of holiness:

> "It is God's will that you should be sanctified: that you should avoid sexual immorality; that each of you should learn to control his own body in a way that is holy and honorable, not in passionate lust like the heathen, who do not know God; and that in this matter no one should wrong his brother or take advantage of him. The Lord will punish men for all such sins, as we have already told you and warned you. For God did not call us to be impure, but to live a holy life. Therefore, he who rejects this instruction does not reject man but God, who gives you his Holy Spirit." (1 Thessalonians 4:3-8)

This runs directly against our culture, which says that sex between consenting adults is okay. We don't have to condemn and put down all those around us who live loosely, but we need to hold high standards for ourselves, and see that our churches hold high standards for members.

Greedy for Sex (5:3)

Ephesians 5:3 extends this farther. Not only sexual immorality but "any kind of impurity or, of greed" are prohibited to Christians. Impurity seems to fit the context well, but greed? Perhaps Paul is using "greed" in a metaphorical sense such as is found in 4:19, "They have given themselves over to sensuality so as to indulge in every kind of impurity, with a continual lust (*pleonexia*) for more" (NIV). Greek *pleonexia* means "greediness, insatiableness, avarice, covetousness," literally, "a desire to have more than

---

[4] *Ibid*. "Prig" means "one who offends or irritates by observance of proprieties (as of speech or manners) in a pointed manner or to an obnoxious degree."

one's due."[5] Usually it is used of money and materialism, and perhaps it is so used here, too, though I think it refers here to insatiability for sex.

Obscenity and Dirty Jokes (5:4)

Verse 4 cautions us about "obscenity,[6] foolish talk or coarse joking." Using the F-word isn't strictly "swearing." Swearing means to take God's name as in an oath, "by God!" But we Christians need to be careful how we express ourselves. We don't have to be prudish or necessarily sober-sided about sex. Nor do we have to constantly complain to others how offended we are by their crude language. But we ourselves must be respectful and clean in our speech. God is fully capable of retraining our mouths if we desire him to. Clean speech is part of the purity that God seeks to lead us into.

Robbing Us of Our Kingdom Inheritance (5:5-6)

Notice the seriousness of Paul's warning:

"For of this you can be sure: No immoral, impure or greedy person ... has any inheritance in the kingdom of Christ and of God. Let no one deceive you with empty words ...." (5:5-6a)

There's a similar solemn warning in 1 Corinthians 6:

"Do you not know that the wicked will not inherit the kingdom of God? Do not be deceived: Neither the sexually immoral nor idolaters nor adulterers, nor male prostitutes nor homosexuals ... will inherit the kingdom of God. *And that is what some of you were*. But you were washed, you were sanctified, you were justified in the name of the Lord Jesus Christ and by the Spirit of our God." (1 Corinthians 6:9-11)

"There's nothing more wrong with sexual sin than any other kind of sin," you'll hear people say. True. But the warnings about it are especially severe. And God's miracles of washing and sanctifying and justifying are especially wonderful. Many of the Christians in Paul's day came out of a life of immorality and afterwards lived a life of purity. God grants the same kind of washing and forgiveness and repentance today!

Q1. (Ephesians 5:2-3) Why does Paul warn so strongly against sexual sin? Is sexuality part of our spiritual life or can it be (should it be) partitioned from our spiritual life?
http://www.joyfulheart.com/forums/index.php?showtopic=544

---

[5] *Pleonexia*, BDAG 824.

[6] "Obscenity" (NIV) and "filthiness" (KJV) is *aischrotēs*, "behavior that flouts social and moral standards, shamefulness, obscenity" (BDAG 29), from *aischunō*, "to shame" or "be ashamed."

Greed for Money (5:5)

Let's look closely at Ephesians 5:5 for a moment. Paul mentions the "greedy person" (*pleonektēs*[7]), and then comments, "such a man is an idolater." An idolater is one who worships a false god. You and I have met people who seem to worship sex – and money. Anything which consumes us so much that we seem to worship it is wrong – unless it is God whom we love with all our heart and soul and mind and strength.

Do you have anything in your life that you love so much that it displaces God and God's work? On Super Bowl Sunday, for example, our values become clear. Where do your values conflict? We are to be worshippers of God, not idolaters.

There was a movement beginning in some of the churches of the Greek empire to treat sexual immorality as a light thing. Scholars call it proto-gnosticism. It was very dualistic. The body is "matter" and therefore bad by definition, these people would teach. The "spirit" is good and holy. Thus, they would reason, it doesn't matter what you do with your body sexually – the body is bad by definition – so long as your spirit is pure. You can see hints of this in 1 Corinthians 6:13 and Revelation 2:14-15, 20-23. Paul says concerning this kind of reasoning, "Let no one deceive you with empty words" (5:6).

From Darkness to Light (5:8-14)

"[8]For you were once darkness, but now you are light in the Lord. Live as children of light [9](for the fruit of the light consists in all goodness, righteousness and truth) [10]and find out what pleases the Lord. [11]Have nothing to do with the fruitless deeds of darkness, but rather expose them. [12]For it is shameful even to mention what the disobedient do in secret. [13]But everything exposed by the light becomes visible, [14]for it is light that makes everything visible. This is why it is said:

'Wake up, O sleeper,
rise from the dead,
and Christ will shine on you.'"(5:8-14)

In a darkening world, Christian purity and faithfulness shine all the brighter. Whereas in the 1950s, America espoused these values culturally, in our day purity and goodness are mocked and caricatured. But in the increasing gloom, Christians shine as "light in the Lord" (5:8).

It is hard for us to stand against our culture, to be counter-cultural. The essence of Christianity is not being counter-cultural, however, but a personal love for the Lord that

---

[7] *Pleonektēs* is from *pleonexia*, "greed," which we looked at in verse 3.

delights in "finding out what pleases the Lord" (5:10). We've had too much negativity in our faith. This is the positive, the seeking, the finding out, the searching to see what pleases God. When we please the Lord, we can have the strength to stand up under pressure.

And pressure there will be, since light by its very nature exposes dark corners. When we live with high moral values we put to shame the actions of others and some of them will hate us for it (while perhaps admiring us at the same time). I don't think that our job is to be society's tattletale, but to be society's example and standard of righteousness.

Ours is a calling to live as light vs. darkness, brilliant light vs. shameless unmentionable sins done in darkness. To conclude this section, Paul quotes what seems to have been a well-known Christian hymn, though we do not have any other extant text of this hymn except the fragment here:

"Wake up, O sleeper,
rise from the dead,
and Christ will shine on you." (5:14)

Just as preachers today quote well-known hymns ("Amazing Grace," etc.), Paul did the same in his day. Every contemporary would recognize the reference for what it is. That's probably what we see here.

Make the Most of Every Opportunity (5:15-16)

"Be very careful, then, how you live – not as unwise but as wise, making the most of every opportunity, because the days are evil." (5:15-16)

In our light-living, then, we are to "be very careful," to be "wise," making the most of every opportunity to shine for God (5:15-16).

Verse 16 is interesting. KJV translates it: "Redeeming the time, because the days are evil." The verb is *exagorazō*, which had commercial uses of "buy, buy up something" and "redeem, buy back." Figuratively it means "to gain something, especially advantage or opportunity, make the most of."[8] This is joined with the noun *kairos*. Greek has two main words for the concept of time: *chronos*, which is used in reference to the stream of time, and *kairos*, which is used of individual periods, points, or moments of time.[9]

So this verse is referring to taking full advantage of every "moment," each "opportunity" which presents itself. The opportunity to do the right thing, to say the appropriate

---

[8] *Exagorazō*, BDAG 343.
[9] Hans-Christoph Hahn, "Time," NIDNTT 3:833-844.

thing, does not come at all times. There are those "teachable moments," those significant times that we are to watch out for and not let slip by due to our timidity or fear.

So this verse is to be translated "making the most of every opportunity" (NIV). Eugene H. Peterson paraphrases it in *The Message* this way:

> "So watch your step. Use your head. Make the most of every chance you get. These are desperate times!"

Q2. (Ephesians 5:15-16) Why does Paul exhort us to make the most of every opportunity? Why do we resist that? What must happen in our lives so we can be ready for the opportunity?
http://www.joyfulheart.com/forums/index.php?showtopic=545

Avoid Drunkenness (5:17-18a)

> "Therefore do not be foolish, but understand what the Lord's will is. Do not get drunk on wine, which leads to debauchery. Instead, be filled with the Spirit." (5:17-18)

"Do not be foolish," Paul continues, "but understand what the Lord's will is" (5:17). Our standard is not what others do, or what we can get away with, but what God's will is.

Paul's society, as ours, was afflicted with drunkenness as an escape. But alcohol and mind-altering drugs while facilitating escapism, dull the believers so they can't "make the most of every opportunity" (5:16)

Paul isn't a teetotaler (1 Timothy 5:23), but he stands firmly against drunkenness. What is drunkenness? A certain blood-alcohol level? The problem with intoxication is three-fold in this context:

1. **Drunkenness leads to "debauchery"** (NIV, RSV), "dissipation" (NASB). The word is Greek *asōtia*, "the character of an *asōtos*, i.e., of an abandoned man, one that cannot be saved,"[10] from *a*, "not" +*sōzō*, "to save." *Asōtia* denotes "wastefulness", then "reckless abandon, debauchery, dissipation, profligacy."[11] So drunkenness leads to moral abandon, it leads people to a place from which they cannot be saved (except by God's grace and power).

---

[10] *Asōtia*, Thayer 82.
[11] *Asōtia*, BDAG, 148.

2. **Drunkenness prevents our light from shining** brightly in the dark world (5:8-14).
3. **Drunkenness dulls our ability to "be careful"** (5:15) and to "make the most of every opportunity (5:16).

In Paul's day drunkenness came primarily from wine and beer. They didn't have distilled spirits in those days. Nor did they have marijuana, cocaine, heroin, crack, or speed. They had wine and beer as intoxicants. We are admonished to avoid intoxication! Rather, we are to seek another kind of intoxicant, another kind of "high," the fullness of the Spirit (5:18).

Q3. (Ephesians 5:17-18) What is the primary temptation involved with drugs and alcohol? How can drug or alcohol use substitute for the "high" of the Spirit? How can being filled with the Spirit help us fend off the temptations of drugs and alcohol?
http://www.joyfulheart.com/forums/index.php?showtopic=546

Be Filled with the Spirit (5:18)

"Do not get drunk on wine, which leads to debauchery. Instead, be filled with the Spirit." (5:18)

Sometimes people can be so overwhelmed by the presence of the Spirit that they appear intoxicated. What happened on the day of Pentecost was one of those occasions.

"All of them were filled with the Holy Spirit and began to speak in other tongues as the Spirit enabled them." (Acts 2:4)

"... Some, however, made fun of them and said, 'They have had too much wine' ... Then Peter stood up... 'These men are not drunk, as you suppose. It's only nine in the morning!'" (Acts 2:13-15)

They were experiencing a kind of ecstasy, a spiritual buoyancy in the Spirit. Being filled with the Spirit, however, is not always ecstatic. While speaking in tongues seems to be associated with ecstasy in Acts 2, in 1 Corinthians 14, people are told to control themselves and their manifestation of the Spirit.[12] An initial experience with the Spirit is sometimes ecstatic, but once we've learned to include the Spirit and his power in our lives, being filled with the Spirit can be wonderful, uplifting, and empowering without

---

[12] For more on this, see my essay, "Spirit Baptism, the New Birth, and Speaking in Tongues," *The Joyful Heart*, January 15, 2000 (www.joyfulheart.com/scholar/spirit-baptism.htm).

being ecstatic. Jesus was certainly filled with the Spirit without ecstasy. This is not to say that there may be times that we will be caught up in ecstasy before the Lord. And when that happens, enjoy the Lord!

Singing to One Another and to God (5:19-20)

> "Speak to one another with psalms, hymns and spiritual songs. Sing and make music in your heart to the Lord, always giving thanks to God the Father for everything, in the name of our Lord Jesus Christ." (5:19-20)

The kind of Spirit-intoxication of which Paul speaks in Ephesians 5:18-20 involves worship and mutual spiritual upbuilding.

- **Psalms** were singing the Psalter, the book of Psalms, which was written to be sung, and was sung by the Jews in Paul's day.
- **Hymns** "probably had a religious and cultic significance ... as a technical term for festive psalms of praise, and for liturgical calls and recitations."[13] Group members were encouraged to each bring a hymn or some other contribution from the Spirit when the believers gathered, in order to build up one another (1 Corinthians 14:16).
- **Spiritual songs** may have been more spontaneous, perhaps like Paul's "singing in the Spirit" (1 Corinthians 14:15), though the lines between psalms, hymns, and spiritual songs are not firmly drawn.

Notice that verse 19a focuses on the effect of our songs on one another, while verse 19b looks at our musical worship as it relates to God. The manner of these Spirit-filled praises is always God-oriented: "Always giving thanks to God the Father for everything, in the name of our Lord Jesus Christ" (6:20). An attitude of thankfulness underlies all true worship.

Q4. (Ephesians 5:19-20) What kind of attitude should underlie our corporate singing? How is corporate singing designed to help us singers? How is it designed to worship God? How does singing in your own daily life help you worship?
http://www.joyfulheart.com/forums/index.php?showtopic=547

---

[13] Karl-Heinz Bartels, "Song, Hymn, Psalm," NIDNTT 3:668-670.

This section spells out the joyful intimacy of walking with the Lord, the relationship we enjoy with our Father and with Christ. Paul exhorts us to:

- Imitate our Father as beloved children (5:1)
- Live as children of light (5:8)
- Learn what pleases the Lord and then do it (5:10)
- Make music in our hearts to the Lord (5:19b)
- Thank God continually in everything (5:20).

What a contrast between the darkness of unbelief and the light and joy that Christians enjoy! We must leave the mental blindness and moral bankruptcy of the Gentiles, Paul says, and instead put on the new self, the purity and light and spirit and joy of the Lord. May this understanding of essential Christianity permeate our churches anew in our day!

Prayer

Father, help us as we learn to walk in light. Help us to surrender to you our desires for sex, for money, and for intoxication. Instead, let us find our "high" in you – knowing you, walking with you, and loving you. Give us a continual attitude of thankfulness, we pray. In Jesus' name. Amen.

Key Verses

"Be imitators of God, therefore, as dearly loved children." (Ephesians 5:1)

"Live as children of light ... and find out what pleases the Lord." (Ephesians 5:8, 10)

"Making the most of every opportunity, because the days are evil." (Ephesians 5:16)

"Be filled with the Spirit. Speak to one another with psalms, hymns and spiritual songs. Sing and make music in your heart to the Lord, always giving thanks to God the Father for everything, in the name of our Lord Jesus Christ." (Ephesians 5:18-20)

13. Christian Husbands and Christian Wives (5:21-33)

This next section of Paul's Letter to the Ephesians (5:21-6:9) deals with proper relationships between people, what German scholars call a *Haustafel* (Table of Household Duties):

- Wives to husbands (5:22-25)
- Husbands to wives (5:26-33)
- Children to parents (6:1-3)
- Fathers to children (6:4)
- Servants to masters (6:5-8)
- Masters to servants (6:9)

The Holy Family also had to work at submission, love, and self-sacrifice. Detail from Bartolomeo Esteban Murillo (1617-1682, "The Holy Family with a Small Bird" (c. 1650), oil on canvas, 144 x 188 cm, Museo del Prado, Madrid.

It is common in our day to dismiss Paul because he doesn't agree with modern ideas of political correctness and feminism. He encourages slaves to obey their masters. How could Paul expect us to take him seriously if he says such things?

Paul lived in a day when Christianity was just seeking to become established in the Mediterranean world. Christians were already considered "atheists" because they refused to worship the Roman and Greek deities. If Paul had encouraged the women to exercise their freedom and the slaves to rebel against their masters, the vital truths of Christianity would have been eclipsed by social and political issues, and the new faith would have been utterly crushed.

If you've studied history, you've learned that you must judge a person's actions by the standards of the society in which he or she lived, not by modern standards, which change every few years, anyway. Don't discount Paul because he lived in a patriarchal society that condoned slavery. If you take the time to see what he is saying, you'll come to realize that his words are indeed revolutionary. In his careful Christian teaching are the seeds of true equality.

Submit Yourselves (5:21)

"Aren't you tired of all these jokes about the President?" asks Jay Leno on "The Tonight Show." "I'm not!" he cracks. And proceeds to tell joke after joke, night after night, degrading our President on television. Whether or not we voted for the President, we must respect him and submit to his authority. If I were to take constant potshots at the President, God would be on my case, since submission to authority is necessary for good order in society, and God did not come to bring chaos and anarchy, but good order (Romans 13:1-6). In a free society I can say nearly anything, but that doesn't make it wise or right. "'Everything is permissible for me' – but not everything is beneficial" (1 Corinthians 6:12).

One of the key words in 5:21-6:9 is "submit." You'll discover that submission is not the same as obedience. Nor does Paul does not teach "chain of command" like some have insisted. Let's see what he does teach.

The Greek verb *hypotassomai* used in the theme verse 21 is used in a reflexive sense, "subject oneself, be subjected or subordinated, obey."[1] *Hypotassomai* is a compound of two words *hypo*, "under" (from which we get our "hypodermic," "under" the skin) + *tassō* "to place, to station, to place in a certain order."[2] Paul is saying, "subject yourself." Rather than teaching rote obedience in action and word, Paul is teaching a voluntary placement of oneself under another "out of reverence for Christ" (vs. 21b).

While this often involves obedience, this is not quite the same as obedience. In Figure 1 you can see that Paul could have used a number of words if he had meant raw obedience here. Instead, he uses *hypotossaomai*, meaning "to subordinate oneself," to voluntarily place oneself under another's authority. This is much different than to unquestioningly obey or to obey only grudgingly. Children are told to obey (6:1). Slaves are told to obey (6.5-6), but wives are told to voluntarily submit to their husbands.[3]

---

[1] *Hypotassō*, BDAG 1042.

[2] *Hypotassō*, Thayer 615.

[3] For a careful study of submission and headship, see my paper, "Headship (*kephalē*) and Submission (*hupotassomai*) in Ephesians 5:21-33." www.jesuswalk.com/ephesians/kephale-headship-ephesians.htm

It is important to note that submission has nothing to do with the inherent worth or value of an individual. Paul teaches equal value and standing before God: "There is neither Jew nor Greek, slave nor free, male nor female, for you are all one in Christ" (Galatians 3:28). Peter teaches that wives and husbands are "joint heirs of the grace of life" (1 Peter 3:7). But to teach

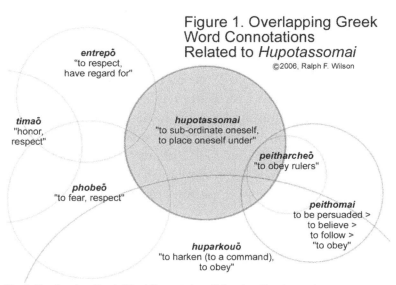

Fig. 1. Overlapping Greek Word Connotations Related to *Hupotassomai*.

that equal value means equal authority is foolish and leads to anarchy. Even in the most egalitarian of societies, we have authority relationships that must be honored to promote good order. Thus the principles Paul teaches here have validity two thousand years later in modern society. They are just applied somewhat differently in different situations and cultures.

Headship (*kephalē*)

"22Wives, submit to your husbands as to the Lord. 23For the husband is the head of the wife as Christ is the head of the church, his body, of which he is the Savior. 24Now as the church submits to Christ, so also wives should submit to their husbands in everything." (5:22-24)

The reason given for a wife to submit to her husband is that he is "the head of the wife as Christ is of the Church" (vs. 23). Those who teach "chain of command" from headship, equate "head" with "boss." In his letters, Paul uses the Greek noun *kephalē*, "head," in a number of ways, some of which overlap, as illustrated in Figure 2:

1. **Origin** (Colossians 1:15, 17, 18; 1 Corinthians 11:3). The theme verse of Ephesians is, "to bring all things in heaven and on earth together under one head, even Christ" (Ephesians 1:10). Christ is the beginning – and the end, and all creation finds

its right place in him. Unity is a strong undercurrent in this verse as well is throughout Ephesians. The idea of "one flesh" in 5:31 is related.

2. **Source, Creator** (Colossians 1:16). We derive our idea of "headwaters" from this concept.
3. **Sustainer** (Ephesians 4:16; 1:23; Colossians 1:17; 2:19).
4. **Source of Growth** (Ephesians 4:15-16; Colossians 2:19)
5. **First in Rank** (Colossians 1:18)
6. **Ruler** (Ephesians 1:20-22; Colossians 1:10). Our "headmaster" carries this idea.[4]

But these concepts are related to Christ's headship, not a husband's, you protest. Perhaps, but 5:23 seems to indicate that "the husband is the head of the wife *as* (in a similar way) Christ is the head of the church." We can't push this to its fullest extent, of course, since husbands aren't divine. But as we will see, they do have many responsibilities towards their wives that relate to the concepts contained in *kephalē*. And nowhere in this passage is "boss" one of those concepts.

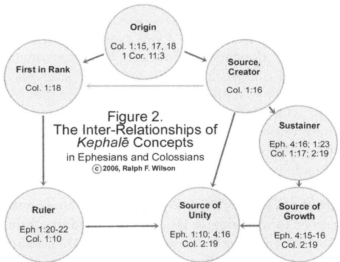

Fig. 2. The Inter-Relationships of *Kephale* Concepts in Ephesians and Colossians.

Verse 24 indicates that "wives should submit to their husbands in everything." This means that in all areas the wife is to let her husband make the final decision. Does this mean she is not to disagree with her husband? By no means!

A wife's particular personality and gifts will be different from her husband's in any given marriage. In her areas of giftedness and strength, she will provide strength to the marriage and leadership in those particular areas.

[4] Ibid.

Submission "As to the Lord" (5:22b)

Just because the husband has final responsibility doesn't make him wise or right or omnipotent. When there is a conflict, the wife must do whatever she can to help him see things from a broader perspective. She must lovingly and submissively correct him when he is wrong, not to put him down (that would be placing herself over him), but to build him up and make him a better man (that is, true servanthood).

What if the husband leads the wife and family to do something stupid? I think submission requires going along.

What if the husband requires the wife to do something illegal, immoral, or which endangers her safety or the safety of the children? According to some teachers I've heard, she can tell God, "I was just following orders." That didn't work as a defense for Nazi war criminals at Nuremberg and it won't work here. To submit to a husband "as to the Lord" means that *the Lord* is the supreme head, and that his commands take precedence over those of a husband when they are in conflict. Sometimes a submissive wife will need to say, "I'm sorry, but I can't in good conscience do that." We can't compromise our faith and conscience to uphold the principle of submission. But, within the wide bounds of a marriage, a wife should be submissive to her husband. So says the Apostle Paul, whom Christ appointed to instruct *His* Church.

Q1. (Ephesians 5:22-24) Why should a wife submit to her husband? According to these verses, to what degree is a wife required to submit to a husband who is not a Christian or who is a carnal Christian? Does submission mean a wife doesn't verbally disagree? What if there's a conflict with the wife's conscience?

http://www.joyfulheart.com/forums/index.php?showtopic=548

Husbands, Give Yourselves Up for Your Wives (5:25-30)

"25Husbands, love your wives, just as Christ loved the church and gave himself up for her 26to make her holy, cleansing her by the washing with water through the word, 27and to present her to himself as a radiant church, without stain or wrinkle or any other blemish, but holy and blameless. 28In this same way, husbands ought to love their wives as their own bodies. He who loves his wife loves himself. 29After all, no one ever hated his own body, but he feeds and cares for it, just as Christ does the church – 30for we are members of his body." (5:25-30)

If you think submission is difficult, wives, look at what Paul says to your husbands: "Love your wives, just as Christ loved the church and gave himself up for her" (vs. 25). Jesus laid down his life for the benefit of the Church. Husbands are to do no less towards their wives – that is, if they are serious about their role as "head."

A lot of men I know are selfish, self-absorbed, and immature. Jesus calls us to grow up. Just as Christ humbled himself before his disciples and washed their feet, so husbands must humble themselves before their wives and family in order to serve them unselfishly. At the Last Supper "a dispute arose among them as to which of them was considered to be greatest." No doubt this was the context of Jesus washing their feet.

> "The kings of the Gentiles lord it over them, and those who exercise authority over them call themselves Benefactors. But you are not to be like that. Instead, the greatest among you should be like the youngest, and the one who rules like the one who serves." (Luke 22:24-27)

In Mark's gospel, this passage concludes with the words:

> "For even the Son of Man did not come to be served, but to serve, and to give his life as a ransom for many." (Mark 10:45)

This is what it means to be head: source, provider, sustainer, source of unity, source of growth. Yes, ruler, too, but only in the context of this service. Our love for our wives is to match Christ's love for his church. Our service to our wives is to match Christ's giving up himself for his church.

Serving the Imperfect Wife (5:26-27)

Notice that Christ's example of service and redemption to an imperfect church is the model for a husband's love:

> "[25]Husbands, love your wives, just as Christ loved the church and gave himself up for her [26]to make her holy, cleansing her by the washing with water through the word, [27]and to present her to himself as a radiant church, without stain or wrinkle or any other blemish, but holy and blameless." (5:25-27)

When we become impatient with our wives, our love needs growing. When our wives make mistakes and show their human imperfections, we must love them as Christ loves us imperfect humans and bears with our weaknesses. How much can we put up with, husbands? Our standard is Christ's love for sinful humanity. And his patient, costly, sacrificial quest finally is bringing about a beautiful, radiant Bride that has been cleansed and is whole. We should not imagine that our love for our wives will require less.

Q2. (Ephesians 5:25-30) Does being head of the wife involve being "boss"? Why or why not? What does being "head" require of a husband? What is the example husbands are to follow in headship?

http://www.joyfulheart.com/forums/index.php?showtopic=549

One Flesh (5:28-32)

Paul sets a very high standard for love, patience, and humble service. Then he gives a second rationale. If you can't love your wife because it is Christ's way, he is saying, then love her for your own benefit:

> "[28]In this same way, husbands ought to love their wives as their own bodies. He who loves his wife loves himself. [29]After all, no one ever hated his own body, but he feeds and cares for it, just as Christ does the church – [30]for we are members of his body. [31]'For this reason a man will leave his father and mother and be united to his wife, and the two will become one flesh.' [32]This is a profound mystery – but I am talking about Christ and the church." (5:28-32)

This passage contains a very simple but very profound concept: "He who loves his wife loves himself" (5:28b). Think about it. Why is it true? Precisely this: "The two will become one flesh" (5:31) quoting Genesis 2:24. Jesus also used this ancient verse to teach on marriage:

> "So they are no longer two, but one. Therefore what God has joined together, let man not separate" (Matthew 19:6).

"Husbands ought to love their wives as their own bodies," says Paul. "He who loves his wife loves himself" (5:28). As a young husband I was off in my world doing my thing, and, sad to say, oblivious to some of my wife's struggles and hurts. In the midst of a real struggle she was having, this passage came home to me. This isn't just her problem, this is mine. We are one. What hurts her, does indeed hurt me. What helps her, does indeed help me. When I began to understand this, I began to take her needs much more seriously and began to love her as head rather than try to make her conform to my wishes that were causing her pain.

Now even this seems kind of selfish: If you want to help yourself, then help your wife. Isn't this just love for our own benefit? I don't think so. True headship must consider the needs of the whole body, not just the needs of the head. "If one part suffers, every part suffers with it" (1 Corinthians 12:26).

Paul is speaking to hard-headed, self-willed husbands like me. He's saying, "You dummy! Don't you realize that you and your wife are one? If you can't treat her right for her sake, then treat her right for your own sake."

Our culture has largely forgotten this truth, and our marriages are suffering for it. We have emphasized each partner's rights and freedoms and self-identity so much, that we have under-emphasized the couple's essential unity, oneness. When we marry we are charting a single course together. We are not going our separate ways while living together for economic convenience and sexual pleasure. We are one, whether we understand it or not. And actions that erode that essential unity work against our marriages. Yes, we are unique individuals, and we must not smother one another and try to suppress one another's uniqueness. But the key to marriage is not our uniqueness. It is the uniting of our uniqueness to be one. The body analogy, which Paul uses in our passage, is apt: respecting our individual functions and gifts, we work for the good of the body, the whole, the one couple, the "corporation." We are truly "one flesh" – that is the core of Paul's teaching here.

Q3. (Ephesians 5:28) In what sense is a husband's care for his wife's needs just common sense in taking care of his own needs? What is the principle from Genesis 2:24 that underlies this?
http://www.joyfulheart.com/forums/index.php?showtopic=550

The Marriage of Christ and His Church (5:32)

"This is a profound mystery – but I am talking about Christ and the church." (5:32)

The theme of unity in Ephesians offers a great deal to help our marriages. Unity and love are the underlying themes of this passage, not "chain of command." But this is bigger than just me and my wife or you and your husband. "This is a profound mystery," says Paul, "but I am talking about Christ and the church" (5:32). The principles which underlie our marriages, also underlie Christ and his church: love, honoring uniqueness, and celebrating unity. We all must voluntarily submit to Christ, whether or not we happen to like it at the time.

Pulling It All Together (5:33)

"However, each one of you also must love his wife as he loves himself, and the wife must respect her husband." (5:33)

This passage began with a call for mutual submission: "Submit to one another out of reverence for Christ" (5:21). The form of our submission may be different as our roles are different. For the wife this submission takes the form of "respect." The Greek noun *phobos*, "fear," carries here the connotation of "reverence, respect."[5] The Christian wife has respect for her husband's role as head and acquiesces to it willingly (5:33). For the husband this submission means loving his wife so much that he gives up his selfishness to help her and strengthen her.

Moving Toward the Ideal

I am inevitably asked, "Am I to submit to my husband if he is a selfish clod who doesn't care for me?" Yes (1 Peter 3:1-6), and your loving submission can cause him to grow in Christ and grow in his love for you. Can you submit to a selfish man because you trust him? No. Only selfless love builds the kind of trust the church has in Jesus. To an immature, selfish man that submission will require great trust in Christ to help in the situation. To a loving, caring, Christian husband, that submission will be more and more from the heart.

"How can I love my wife and care for her when she is bossy and bitchy?" You are to love her in spite of herself, just as Christ loved us in spite of ourselves, and gave himself up on the cross to free us from our sins. Only Christ's love for an imperfect church could have brought about her cleansing, perfection, and wholeness.

Q4. (Ephesians 5:32) In what sense is Christ our Husband as individuals? As a church? What are the implications of this for our lives? What does this say about Christ's responsibilities towards us?
http://www.joyfulheart.com/forums/index.php?showtopic=551

Ephesians 5:21-33 is an ideal, of course, not where we start, but where we are headed. This is not a scripture to use to beat over your wife's or husband's head, but for us as individuals to learn from and pattern our own lives after. To the degree that a husband is loving and trustworthy, a wife is able to submit more fully and trustingly. To the degree that a wife is loving and submissive, a husband can care for her and lead the family to a better way of life. As we imperfect spouses stop blaming our mates and seek to be what *we* are supposed to be in Christ, then – gradually – Christ can bring about the

[5] *Phobos*, BDAG 1062.

beautiful marriage that Paul describes here, a marriage that patterns itself after the marriage of Christ and his church.

Prayer

Father, we fall so short of this ideal of Christian marriage. Please help us to develop a heart of love so that this can work in our lives and in our marriages. Teach us to submit. Teach us to give of ourselves sacrificially. And forgive us when we fail. In Jesus' name, we pray. Amen.

Key Verses

"Wives, submit to your husbands as to the Lord." (Ephesians 5:22)

"Husbands, love your wives, just as Christ loved the church and gave himself up for her." (Ephesians 5:25)

"In this same way, husbands ought to love their wives as their own bodies. He who loves his wife loves himself." (Ephesians 5:28)

14. Children and Parents, Employers and Employees (6:1-9)

This passage continues Paul's instructions on how to "Submit to one another out of reverence for Christ" (5:21). First, he discusses the delicate relationship between wives and husbands (5:22-33). Now he turns to the submission of children to their parents.

Children Obey Your Parents (6:1-3)

> "¹Children, obey your parents in the Lord, for this is right. ²'Honor your father and mother' –which is the first commandment with a promise – ³'that it may go well with you and that you may enjoy long life on the earth.'" (6:1-3)

Childhood is a period of constant testing of the limits. Of "psyching out" parents. Of wheedling. Of manipulating. Of learning to get one's own way. Yes, there are some children who are completely passive and let life happen to them all their lives. But most are pushing, testing. And that is how it should be. That is how growth takes place and maturity gradually takes the place of youthful stupidity.

In the Bible we see Joseph as both child and father, slave and master. James Jacques Joseph Tissot (French painter and illustrator, 1836-1902), "Pharaoh welcoming Joseph's Family to Egypt" (1896-1900), watercolor, The Jewish Museum, New York.

But in the midst of this intensely active period, God gives one clear command to children: "Obey your parents in the Lord, for this is right." The verb "obey" is *hypakouō* comes from the root *akouō*, "listen." *Hypakouō* builds on this by combining the concept of *listening* with *harkening to* or *responding to a command*, "to obey."[1] Notice that this obedience is "in the Lord," that is, obedience to parents is part of our obedience to the

---

[1] Gerhard Kittel, *akouō, ktl.*, TDNT 1:216-225.

Lord. If my parent asks me to do something immoral, my first obligation would be to obey the Lord instead of my parent.

Honor Your Father and Mother

Paul supports his command to obey with several buttresses:

First, the command to obey one's parents is Number Five of the Ten Commandments – "Honor your father and mother." Paul is paraphrasing the form of the command given in Deuteronomy 5:16. Obedience to parents is not only a manmade rule, it is given by God, to be built into the very fabric of our values.

"Honor" is *timaō*, from the idea of "to value, to deem worthy," then "to honor."[2] Certainly we are to honor our parents when we are children under their care. But it doesn't stop there. Jesus quotes the Fifth Commandment when he castigates the Pharisees for creating legal ways to evade supporting their parents when they were aged (Mark 7:9-13). Proverbs is full of admonitions to honor parents both as children (Proverbs 1:8-9; 15:5) and as adults (Proverbs 20:20; 23:22-25; 28:24; 30:11, 17). We have a duty to honor, listen to, and care for them that extends beyond childhood.

But here Paul is admonishing children still at home. Why does he emphasize obeying and honoring parents? Because children have a natural tendency to ignore what parents say and do their own thing.

Promises to the Obedient

The command comes with two promises:

"That it may go well with you ..." is self-evident. Those who obey their parents stay out of trouble a lot better than those who don't. Childhood and teen years are a very self-righteous time. *We* know what's best. How could parents know?

I remember when I was in high school having heated arguments with my Dad at the dinner table about politics and issues of the day. I was very passionate in my arguments and he was equally strong in his. It surprised me, a month later, when discussing the subject with my friends that I was taking my Dad's position instead of the one which I had so hotly contended for. My sense of right and good still needed molding by his wiser insights. I thank God for my Dad. When I obeyed him, things went better for me.

The second part of the promise is more serious yet: **"... that you may enjoy long life on the earth."** Obedience to our parents is an invaluable protection that will increase our lifespan. If we don't learn from our parents how to get along with people, we can get

---

[2] Johannes Schneider, *timē, ktl.*, TDNT 7:169-180.

killed. The culture of our inner cities is no less violent that that of Old Testament days. Obedience to our parents will keep us alive, now and in the future. It will also help us earn a living so we have enough food to stay alive. Our lifespan is directly dependent upon our willingness to obey.

For children to obey – and for parents to enforce obedience – is sometimes difficult. But children learn in "the school of the home" the vital ability to submit their wills to another. How can a child who doesn't learn to obey a *parent* when wills conflict, ever learn to obey *God* when self-will is propelling him beyond God's limits? Parents have a sacred task to teach obedience, for their children's spiritual *and* physical lives are at stake. Obedience to parents is directly transferred to obedience to our Heavenly Father.

> "Do not withhold discipline from a child," the Proverbs instruct us. "If you punish him with the rod, he will not die. Punish him with the rod and save his *soul* from death" (Proverbs 23:13-14).

At what point does the command to obey our parents give way to the underlying command to honor them? From the very beginning of the Bible we read, "For this reason a man will leave his father and mother and be united to his wife, and they will become one flesh" (Genesis 2:24). There is a time of forming a new family, of leaving the old. At that point the obligation of *obedience* becomes obsolete. But we are always to *honor* our parents and care for them. We have that obligation until death.

Q1. (Ephesians 6:1-3) What kind of obedience and honor is appropriate for adult children to show towards their parents? What might be the exceptions? How do respect and forgiveness figure in this relationship?
http://www.joyfulheart.com/forums/index.php?showtopic=552

Fathers (6:4)

> "Fathers, do not exasperate your children; instead, bring them up in the training and instruction of the Lord." (6:4)

Just because we are parents, however, does not give us the right to rule with the "divine right of kings." Yes, parents are to enforce discipline in the home, but they are to do so wisely.

"Fathers, do not exasperate your children" (vs. 4a, NIV) or "provoke" them (KJV, NRSV). The verb Paul uses is Greek *parorgizō*, "make angry,"[3] "to rouse to wrath, to provoke, exasperate, anger."[4] Of course, when wills clash there is anger. That's a given. But Paul is directing fathers not to deliberately provoke anger by badgering or turning an incident into a power game. This is a fine line and it has to do with a father's own humility and attitude. Fathers who try constantly to make themselves feel better at the expense of their children are neurotic. While anger is part of a conflict of wills, fathers are not to enflame it needlessly.

A closely related passage offers some insight:

> "Fathers, do not embitter (*erethizō*) your children, or they will become discouraged (*athumeō*)." (Colossians 3:21, NIV)

Erethizō means "to cause someone to react in a way that suggests acceptance of a challenge, arouse, provoke," mostly in a bad sense, "irritate, embitter."[5] Purposely provoking our children doesn't produce good fruit. The result is either outright rebellion or discouragement.

Athumeō means "to become disheartened to the extent of losing motivation, be discouraged, lose heart, become dispirited."[6] The word is compounded from the prefix *a*, which means "not" + *thumos*, "spirit, courage." The idea is "to be disheartened, dispirited, broken in spirit."[7]

The purpose of discipline is training and directing the child's spirit, not breaking that tender spirit. Of course, not only fathers, but mothers, too, must keep themselves in check, so that in their diligence to discipline they do not bring hurt.

Training and Instruction (6:4b)

The alternative to provoking the child only to crush him is a very positive commission to parents:

> "Bring them up in the training (*paideia*) and instruction (*nouthesia*) of the Lord" (NIV) or "the nurture and admonition of the Lord." (KJV, 6:4b)

The Greek noun *paideia* (from which we get our words "pedagogy" and "pediatrics") means "upbringing, training, instruction," chiefly attained by "discipline, correction."[8]

---

[3] *Parorgizō*, BDAG 780.
[4] *Parorgizō*, Thayer 490.
[5] *Erethizō*, BDAG 391.
[6] *Athumeō*, BDAG 25.
[7] *Athumeō*, Thayer 14.
[8] *Paideia*, BDAG 748-749.

Nouthesia means "counsel about avoidance or cessation of an improper course of conduct, admonition, instruction, warning."[9] Both of these words can include punishment, but that is not their thrust. "Training and instruction" involve example, maintaining discipline, diligence, teaching, instructing, showing, giving responsibilities, and then supporting them as they learn to keep them faithfully. Warning and admonition are included, too, along with correction.

But what makes this particularly Christian rather than merely parental are the words "in the Lord." Our "training and instruction" are part of our service to Christ. Our children belong to God and we are raising them for *him*. We are told to "bring them up (*ektrephō*) in the Lord." *Ektrephō* means "to provide food, nourish," then "to bring up from childhood, rear."[10] We are to "nourish" our children in the Lord.

So to children Paul says: obey your parents. To parents he says: train and instruct your children in Christ without breaking their spirit.

Q2. (Ephesians 6:4) What kind of behavior by fathers (or mothers, for that matter) can embitter or cause a child to lose heart? What do you think the "training and instruction of the Lord" involves?
http://www.joyfulheart.com/forums/index.php?showtopic=553

Slaves (Employees) (6:5-8)

"[5]Slaves, obey your earthly masters with respect and fear, and with sincerity of heart, just as you would obey Christ. [6]Obey them not only to win their favor when their eye is on you, but like slaves of Christ, doing the will of God from your heart. [7]Serve wholeheartedly, as if you were serving the Lord, not men, [8]because you know that the Lord will reward everyone for whatever good he does, whether he is slave or free." (6:5-8)

The Bible does not promote slavery as American Southern plantation owners believed a century and a half ago, so let's not import that understanding of slavery into Paul's words here. If you look carefully, you'll see the seeds of full freedom and equality (though I won't discuss that topic here). Rather, Paul is dealing with slavery as a fact of life among the people to whom he was ministering.

In the Mediterranean world of Paul's day there were citizens, freedmen, and slaves. And a great many of the people most open to the Christian message were the poor and

---

[9] *Nouthesia*, BDAG 679.
[10] *Ektrephō*, BDAG 311.

oppressed – slaves. If Paul had taught slaves that they were free, and enflamed them to rise up against their slaveowners, as John Brown did just before the American Civil War, the message of the Gospel would have been eclipsed by the issue of slavery. Instead, Paul teaches Christians how to live within the evil system in which they find themselves.

I've found it profitable in our day to substitute the word "employee" for "slave," and "employer" for "master" (*kyrios*), though they aren't fully equivalent. But the instruction Paul would bring in our situation of employees and employers would be very similar. These are his instructions:

Obedience (*hupakouō*, as in 6:1). Employees are to do what their employers tell them to. Notice that Paul says "earthly masters." He is reminding the slaves that it will not always be so. Their masters are only in power here on earth and their authority is neither universal nor eternal.

Respect. The obedience is not just to be to the letter of the employer's directives, but is to include respect, literally "fear and trembling." This isn't cowering terror, but respect. The phrase refers to "a proper spirit of Christian reverence,"[11] "an attitude of due reverence and awe in the presence of God, a godly fear of the believer in view of the final day."[12] We are to be God-fearers and to show due respect for our employers. We are not to despise them in our hearts; we are not to hate the boss. Notice how Paul brings attitude in, rather than mere legalism.

Sincerity of Heart (NIV), literally "singleness of heart" (NRSV, cf. KJV). The word here is *haplotēs*, used of personal integrity expressed in word or action, "simplicity, sincerity, uprightness, frankness."[13] More than respect, we are to offer conscientious, careful service. Years ago, Avis rental cars launched its "We're number 2, we try harder" advertising campaign to get people to switch from Hertz. Service, they were saying, is better when it is motivated by the right attitude. "Sincerity of heart" is the flip side of "eye-service" (6:6).

As to Christ. Sometimes it's hard to see our work as direct service to Christ. But it is vital that we bring our love for Christ right into the midst of every important relationship of our lives, and work is certainly one of those. We are to serve our employers with the same attitude with which we serve Jesus. Our conscientious work is part of our service to Christ, whether we are slaves, or employees, or entrepreneurs serving clients.

[11] Bruce, p. 400, fn. 18.
[12] O'Brien, p. 450.
[13] *Haplotēs*, BDAG 104, 1.

Not with "eyeservice as menpleasers" (KJV). NRSV renders it, "... not only while being watched, and in order to please them...." The NIV puts it, "... not only to win their favor when their eye is on you...." "Oops! The boss is coming. Don't let him see you doing that." Christians are to be faithful to their employers even when no one is there to see. Our Christian work ethic is based on integrity, not impressing the right people.

As Servants of Christ. We are Christ's representatives, no getting around it. When we work, we work as Christ's servants. Our labor may "belong" to our master or our employer, but our underlying motivation is not just money, but "as servants of Christ."

Doing the Will of God from the Heart. Here is heart attitude again. God not only wants to change our actions; he wants to change our attitudes as well.

But what if our employer asks us to do something illegal, immoral, or sleazy? Are we to obey? No, at the cost of our jobs sometimes we must be servants of Christ first, and then servants of our employers second. They don't pay us enough to compromise our consciences.

We can leave and hopefully find another job. Just think how hard it was for a slave to stand up for his or her faith when commanded to compromise! We must be careful to choose our battles wisely, however. Some issues aren't worth dying for, but others are vitally important to our integrity.

As If You Were Serving the Lord, Not Men. A few years ago, a man objected to me quoting a Bible verse in my free business e-mail newsletter. "Religion and business shouldn't mix," he said. I strongly disagree. No, we normally can't be overtly evangelizing on our employer's time. But we are to bring our Christianity all the way into our businesses. If business does not mix with religion, then it rapidly becomes greedy, exploitive, and oppressive. Your employer may be paying you for your time, but all the time you are at work, you are to work "as if you were serving the Lord, not men." It's an attitude thing. It also relates to our understanding of our true reward.

Knowing that the Lord Will Reward. Our employers may be mystified by our good nature and faithful, conscientious service. But God will be pleased and will reward us for our faithfulness to our employers. (And, conversely, punish us for defrauding and despising our employers.) Paul uses the verb *komizō*, here, "receive as recompense,"[14] to contrast man's wages with God's eternal reward.

---

[14] *Komizō*, BDAG 557.

Q3. (Ephesians 6:5-8) What are the characteristics called for in a truly Christian employee, according to Ephesians 6:5-8? How can these attitudes help us in difficult work situations?

http://www.joyfulheart.com/forums/index.php?showtopic=554

Masters, Employers (6:9)

> "And masters, treat your slaves in the same way. Do not threaten them, since you know that he who is both their Master and yours is in heaven, and there is no favoritism with him." (6:9)

Employers are to treat their employees with the same kind of respect, faithfulness, integrity that God expects of employees.

Some employers rule by threats and carry them out ruthlessly. The better ones, however, lead by example and from a position of respect. Yes, they may need to exercise discipline from time to time (Proverbs 29:21). They may need to fire or let an employee go (one of the hardest tasks employers have to do!), but they must do it with honesty, justice, and integrity.

To masters (and employers) who have lost perspective, Paul gives two warnings:

1. **You have a Master in heaven who will hold you to account**. You cannot be an absolute tyrant, you yourself are under God's authority. You may be a master (*kyrios*), in a position of authority, here. But ultimately you are a servant of your Heavenly Master (*kyrios*), and are just as accountable as your slaves or employees.

2. **God shows no favoritism in his judgment**. "Respect of persons" (KJV), "partiality" (NRSV), and "favoritism" (NIV) is *prosōpolēmpsia*, "partiality, the fault of one who when called on to requite or to give judgment has respect to the outward circumstances of men and not to their intrinsic merits, and so prefers, as the more worthy, one who is rich, high-born, or powerful, to another who is destitute of such gifts." [15] God will not give you a better reward because of your "class" or "station" than he will a slave or employee. He expects exactly the same kind of behavior of each of you. You will be judged by how you have acted in this life, not by the position you held.

---

[15] *Prosōpolēmpsia*, Thayer 551.

The Bible has much to say about God's requirements for employers – considerateness (Leviticus 25:42); justice and fair pay for poor and immigrant workers (Deuteronomy 24:14; Proverbs 22:16; Malachi 3:5), prompt and full payment of wages (Deuteronomy 24:15; Leviticus 19:13; Romans 4:4; James 5:4), payment of decent and fair wages (Matthew 10:10; Luke 10:7; 1 Timothy 5:18), and days off for rest (Deuteronomy 5:14). If you are an employer – or on a church board that sets salaries and working conditions for your pastor or church employees – God holds you responsible for how you act towards those over whom he has placed you.

Q4. (Ephesians 6:9) How should Christian employers conduct themselves towards their employees? How should church boards conduct themselves towards church employees? How do you determine a just wage – not merely the one you think you can afford?
http://www.joyfulheart.com/forums/index.php?showtopic=555

This concludes Paul's teaching on submission which began in 5:21. Marriage has its moments of despair for both husbands and wives. No one said that being a parent or child is easy. Being a faithful employee or a fair employer is fraught with frustration and difficulty, as well. But *in* our respective roles, God expects us to live as *his* servants, with our hearts and attitudes trained by *his* Spirit. Only as Christ's life is being worked out in our own are we fully and truly Christian.

Prayer

Father, we find ourselves as both children and parents, and in the various seasons of our lives as both employers and employees. Help us to live out our lives for you with joy and integrity no matter where you have placed us for now. Lord, I'm inclined to complain about my circumstances and whine. Forgive me. Help me to live and serve as part of my service to you. And thank you for your immense grace towards me and each of us. In Jesus' name, I pray. Amen.

Key Verses

"Children, obey your parents in the Lord, for this is right." (Ephesians 6:1)

"Fathers, do not exasperate your children; instead, bring them up in the training and instruction of the Lord." (Ephesians 6:4)

"Serve wholeheartedly, as if you were serving the Lord, not men, because you know that the Lord will reward everyone for whatever good he does, whether he is slave or free." (Ephesians 6:7-8)

15. Wrestling with the Enemy of Our Souls (6:10-18)

"When you become a Christian," say some, "all your troubles are over. God smoothes out all the troubles and life is easier."

"When you become a Christian," say others, "your troubles are just beginning. Satan didn't bother with you before, since you were on his side. Not he will buffet you unmercifully. Fasten your seat belts."

Both are distortions of the truth, which is this: Before you were a Christian, whole areas of your life was devastated because of the way you lived, as well as from the emptiness and purposeless in your life. Now that you have become a Christian, God is renewing your mind and helping you to change your lifestyle. This in itself will save you from a lot of troubles. You now have the Holy Spirit within you to guide and teach and comfort you. You are a lot better off.

But you will face some terrible conflicts ahead. Before you were a Christian, you just gave into the temptations and then suffered the consequences of your sins. Now as you begin to stand against those temptations, you are beginning to realize the real source of them – Satan himself. This struggle against temptation and evil is not against people. It

Gravestone of a Marcus Favonius, a Roman centurion of the 20th Legion (died after 43 AD), Colchester Castle Museum, England.

is against the unseen evil spiritual world of the demonic. But you can stand your ground when you equip yourself with the tools God has given you.

In this passage, Paul spells out for the Ephesians the nature of the battle and describes how to find the strength to resist the temptations we will face.

Relying on God's Strength (6:10-11a)

> "Finally, be strong in the Lord and in his mighty power. Put on the full armor of God so that you can take your stand against the devil's schemes." (6:10-11)

So often we are overcome with a feeling of powerlessness. Much of powerlessness – not all – comes from not using what God has provided. The command in verse 10 is "Be strong[1] in the Lord and in his mighty[2] power."[3] Our problem is that we try to be strong in ourselves, and have not learned the secret of drawing our strength from God.

Paul was afflicted with some kind of disease, it appears from 2 Corinthians 12:7-10. What it was we do not know, though he called it "a thorn in my flesh" and recognized its source: "a messenger of Satan to torment me." Paul didn't sanctify his illness, even though God was using this evil thing, he asked for God to remove it. But God denied his request and instead told him, "My grace is sufficient for you, for my power is made perfect in weakness." God used evil for good once again (Romans 8:28), so that Paul would remain humble and so that he would learn in his weakness to draw on God's strength. Paul learned to glory in it, "For when I am weak," he said, "then I am strong."

Not that he wasn't tested. In 2 Corinthians 11:23-33 he enumerates some of his trials: prison, severe floggings, shipwreck, betrayal, hunger, the pressure of his responsibilities.

> "We are hard pressed on every side, but not crushed; perplexed, but not in despair; persecuted, but not abandoned; struck down, but not destroyed." (2 Corinthians 4:8-9)

To the Philippian church he wrote,

> "I know what it is to be in need, and I know what it is to have plenty. I have learned the secret of being content in any and every situation, whether well fed or hungry, whether living in plenty or in want. I can do[4] everything through him who gives me strength!"[5] (Philippians 4:12-13)

Indeed, the secret is to "be strong *in the Lord* and in *his* mighty power" (6:10). Paul likens it to the armor (and armament) of a soldier, perhaps using one of his prison guards as a model as he penned these lines. "Put on[6] the full armor of God so that you

---

[1] *Endynamoō*, "to become able to function or do something, become strong" (BDAG 333).

[2] *Kratos*, "ability to exhibit or express resident strength, might," here "of intensity in might" (BDAG 565, 1b).

[3] *Ischus*, "capability to function effectively, strength, power, might" (BDAG 484).

[4] *Ischuō*, "to have requisite personal resources to accomplish something, have power, be competent, be able" (BDAG 484).

[5] *Endynamoō*, see note above on Ephesians 6:10.

[6] *Endyō*, "put on, clothe oneself in, wear" (BDAG 333-334), which we saw in 4:24 – "Put on the new self...."

can take your stand against the devil's schemes." When we do not rely on God's strength, we have not donned the full "armor"[7] which he gives us for the struggle.

The Diabolical Nature of the Struggle (6:11b-12)

> "[11]Put on the full armor of God so that you can take your stand against the devil's schemes.[8] [12]For our struggle is not against flesh and blood, but against the rulers, against the authorities, against the powers of this dark world and against the spiritual forces of evil in the heavenly realms." (6:11-12)

Most of us in Western cultures grew up with a scientific, materialist mindset. If you cannot see it or touch it or measure it in a scientific manner, then it is not real. Science has made great strides in the last few decades in "seeing" particles so small they once eluded our electron microscopes, as well as heavenly bodies so far away that we couldn't find them with our finest telescopes, though they were huge.

But there are some things which science is not equipped to measure. Love, for one. Right and wrong, for another. Science can measure the physiological responses to fear, but it cannot "see" fear.

The place where you are reading this, this very moment, is being penetrated by all kinds of waves and signals –TV, radio, microwave. But you can't hear or see them unless you turn on a listening or viewing device. Spiritual beings are the same way. While we can't "see" spiritual beings, we can sense them so long as we have our antennae up.

"I believe in Jesus," I've heard people exclaim, "but I don't believe in Satan and demons." Interesting, since Jesus had a great deal to say about both. That kind of in-your-face ignorance is like a blind man denying the existence of street lights.

In case we didn't know, Paul instructs us on the nature of our spiritual struggle in 6:11b-13:

- The devil's schemes
- Not flesh and blood
- Rulers
- Authorities
- Powers of this dark world
- Spiritual forces of evil in the heavenly realms
- Day of evil

---

[7] *Panoplia*, "the complete equipment of a heavy-armed soldier, full armor" (BDAG 754), from *hoplon*, "implement, weapon," and *pan*, "all."

[8] *Methodeia*, "scheming, craftiness" (Ephesians 4:14; 6:11) (BDAG 625).

Now for a few definitions of the Greek words which underlie our English translations:

"Devil" translates Greek *diabolos* (from which we get words such as "diabolical"): 1. *adj.* "slanderous", 2. *noun,* "one who engages in slander," in the New Testament the title of the principal transcendent evil being "the adversary, the devil."[9] The proper name Satan (which is not used here) is a transliteration of the Hebrew word *satan* meaning "adversary," and in the Bible, in a very special sense, the enemy of God, simply "Satan, the Enemy."[10] The word *diabolos* is used synonymously with *satan* in Revelation 2:9-10 and 20:2.

"Rulers" (NIV, NRSV) and "principalities" (KJV) translate Greek *archē* (from which we get words such as "archbishop") which means "ruler, authority, official."[11] It can be used of good rulers as well as bad. The idea here is that some of the "rulers" in the spiritual realm are demonic in their allegiance. We believe (though the scripture is pretty silent here) that Satan was once an archangel who rebelled against God and was thrown, with the angels under his authority (perhaps a third of heaven's angels), out of heaven (Revelation 12). We call these rebel angels "demons" or "evil spirits," though that terminology was mainly used by Jesus in the Gospels, not so much in Paul's writings.

We see in a hint of this in Daniel 10:12-13, 20, where Daniel relates an experience in which Michael the archangel was delayed in answering Daniel's prayer because of a battle with "the prince of the Persian kingdom." Peter Wagner and others in the intercessory prayer movement in the US believe that spiritual rulers seek to control and influence neighborhoods, cities, regions, and countries. Wagner reports local spiritual breakthroughs in response to prayer directed against the ruling spirits of an area.[12]

"Authorities" (NIV, NRSV) and "powers" (KJV) translate the plural of Greek *exousia,* a generic word meaning "the right to control or command, authority, absolute authority, warrant," both good and bad.[13] When the words *archē* and *exousia* ("principalities and powers") are used together in the New Testament, they always refer to the evil spiritual powers (1 Corinthians 15:24; Ephesians 1:21; 3:10; 6:12; Colossians 1:16, 2:10, 15; 1 Peter 3:22).

---

[9] *Diabolos,* BDAG 226-227.

[10] *Satan,* BDAG 916-917.

[11] *Archē,* BDAG 137-138.

[12] See C. Peter Wagner, *Engaging the Enemy: How to Fight and Defeat Territorial Spirits* (Regal Books, 1991) and C. Peter Wagner and F. Douglas Pennoyer (eds.), *Wrestling with Dark Angels: Toward a Deeper Understanding of the Supernatural Forces in Spiritual Warfare* (Regal Books, 1990).

[13] *Exousia,* BDAG 352-353.

"Powers of this ... world" (NIV), "cosmic powers" (NRSV) or "rulers ... of this world" (KJV) is Greek *kosmokratōr* which means "world-ruler." But the world here is described as "darkness," in other words, Paul is describing here the "rulers of this sinful world."[14]

"Spiritual forces (of evil)" (NIV, NRSV) or "spiritual (wickedness in high places)" (KJV) is Greek *pneumatikos*, "pertaining to the spirit, spiritual," here pertaining to evil spirits.[15] Notice the words to which "spiritual" is appended: "evil" and "heavenly realms" (*epouranos*, "heavenly"). Since Hitler's day it is common to hear people try to make Paul's words refer to the evil social structures of the day – institutionalized evil – and translate the Greek word *epouranos* as "high places," but this doesn't really fit the context here. (Though there is such a thing as institutionalized evil that must be resisted!) We have seen the word "heavenly realms" (*epouranos*) used a number of times in Ephesians, always concerning spiritual realities (Ephesians 1:3, 20; 2:6; 3:10; 6:12). Paul is speaking here about spiritual wickedness in the unseen but very real spiritual sphere in which we presently dwell.

Q1. (Ephesians 6:11-13) Why is it difficult to believe in the devil and demons in our day? How does their existence help explain the struggle humans face on earth? With all their power, how do we stand a chance? Did "the devil make me do it"? What kinds of things *can't* we blame on the demonic?
http://www.joyfulheart.com/forums/index.php?showtopic=556

Stand Your Ground (6:13)

Our problem is that we don't see the spiritual realm and often misunderstand the very nature of the life and death struggle in which we as humans are engaged. It's easy to focus on people as evil. Often they are. But the real struggle is not with the people themselves ("flesh and blood"), but with the evil spiritual forces that are motivating them. If we fight the people, we lose. If we try to fight with intellectual or psychological or metaphysical weapons we will lose. But if we will arm ourselves with God's weapons and fight they way he instructs us, we can succeed.

> "Therefore put on the full armor of God, so that when the day of evil comes, you may be able to stand your ground, and after you have done everything, to stand." (6:13)

---

[14] *Kosmokratōr*, BDAG 561.
[15] *Pneumatikos*, BDAG 837.

What is victory? Is it to swashbuckle our way across the hoards of hell and capture Satan himself? No. But it certainly is to remain standing at the end of the battle.

On Sunday I asked an elderly gentleman at church, "How are you?" and he replied, "I'm still vertical." That's the idea. That is victory: to hold our ground, to stand our ground, not to give in, not to give up. To remain standing at the end of the conflict.

If Satan can discourage us, wear us down, we may fall, we may retreat, we may give up. But victory is to remain, to stand, to be left standing at the end of the day.

One of my interests is American Civil War history, especially the mighty battles of Gettysburg, Antietam, and Sharpsburg. The army that was left standing in possession of the battlefield at the end of the day *was* the victor, even though it may have been wounded and took serious casualties. The armor of God is designed to help us to stand. Jesus said,

> "In the world you shall have tribulation: but be of good cheer; I have overcome the world." (John 16:33, KJV)

Q2. (Ephesians 6:13) What is difficult about standing our ground in today's world? In what way can standing our ground be considered victory? Why are the saints in Revelation 12:11 considered victorious over the devil? How did they stand their ground?
http://www.joyfulheart.com/forums/index.php?showtopic=557

The Nature of the Armament (6:14-17)

> "¹⁴Stand firm then, with the belt of truth buckled around your waist, with the breastplate of righteousness in place, ¹⁵and with your feet fitted with the readiness that comes from the gospel of peace. ¹⁶In addition to all this, take up the shield of faith, with which you can extinguish all the flaming arrows of the evil one. ¹⁷Take the helmet of salvation and the sword of the Spirit, which is the word of God."(6:14-17)

Let's look at the pieces of the armor Paul describes as he develops this military analogy:

Belt of Truth (6:14a)

> "Stand firm then, with the belt of truth buckled around your waist..." (6:14a)

First, the belt[16] of truth. Think of the wide belt that the weight lifter wears to protect and strengthen him.

"If you hold to my teaching," Jesus said, "you are really my disciples. Then you will know the truth, and the truth will set you free" (John 8:31-32). When we don't know any better, the "father of lies," the "great deceiver" can hoodwink us and get the better of us. But when we hold firmly to the truth that we know and seek diligently to acquire wisdom, we are protected. This is a good piece of equipment to put on in the morning with a regular reading of the Scriptures.

Breastplate of Righteousness (6:14b)

"... With the breastplate of righteousness in place..." (6:14b)

The steel, leather, or coat of mail breastplate (*thorax*[17]) of the Roman soldier protected the torso in the thick of battle. Our protection is righteousness. This is two-fold. First, we have been *made* righteous by Christ's death on our behalf (imputed righteousness). We are "holy," "set apart," we are "saints," we belong to God *now*. His righteousness is our righteousness, and his blood covers our sins. We can often be fooled when Satan reminds us of our sins and weaknesses, and tells us, "You've done it now! God will never forgive you after this." Our protection is our understanding of the righteousness in which we stand *in Christ*.

But this righteousness must not be only *imputed* righteousness from Christ. We are also protected by living holy lives, by obedience, by walking in God's ways righteously. When we do that we deprive the devil of a "foothold" (Ephesians 4:27) from which to attack us further. Our righteous ways are a powerful protection from the destruction that sin brings with it.

Q3. (Ephesians 6:14) Why are such simple things as truth and personal holiness such powerful armament? Are they defensive or offensive weapons?
http://www.joyfulheart.com/forums/index.php?showtopic=558

Footgear for Battle (6:15)

"... With your feet fitted with the readiness that comes from the gospel of peace." (6:15)

---

[16] *Zōnnumi*, "to gird. "The girdle is an item of military equipment, e.g., as a broad leather band for protection, as an apron under the armor, as a belt studded with metal, or as a sign of rank" (Albrecht Oepke, *hoplon, ktl.*, TDNT 5:292-315).

[17] *Thorax*, ibid.

Strong footgear[18] is important in a battle situation. If we wear thongs on our feet instead of Army-issue boots, we may slip in the struggle, and leave ourselves exposed to the enemy. But notice that shod feet are also an offensive weapon, an enablement for us to be ready to run with and share the gospel of peace. Truth and good news are a weapon in that they give us sure footing against darkness, deceit, and despair.

> "How beautiful on the mountains are the feet of those who bring good news, who proclaim peace, who bring good tidings, who proclaim salvation, who say to Zion, 'Your God reigns!'" (Isaiah 52:7)

Q4. (Ephesians 6:15) What would be the characteristic of a person who *didn't* have his feet ready to run with the Gospel? How does heart preparation make you more ready to share the Good News with those around you? How does this help defeat the dominion of darkness?

http://www.joyfulheart.com/forums/index.php?showtopic=559

The Shield of Faith (6:16)

> "In addition to all this, take up the shield[19] of faith, with which you can extinguish all the flaming arrows of the evil one." (6:16)

Often before battle, soldiers would soak their leather shields in the local creeks. This made them much heavier, but made them impervious to the flaming arrows shot by the enemy. A shield is both a defensive weapon to hide behind as well as an offensive weapon, which enables you to strike with your sword hand while protecting your body with the shield held in the other.

Sometimes we have devastating circumstances that come upon us like a flaming arrow and threaten to consume us, our family, and our whole position in life. We can react with fear and terror. Or we can put up the shield of faith and start to trust God when all hell breaks loose. Your faith helps you to stand in the intense battles within your mind as well as in your home and workplace. Trust God no matter what is going

---

[18] *Hypodeō*, "to furnish with footgear." "The Roman legionnaires wear half-boots with strong soles." Ibid.

[19] *Thyros*, "probably a long oblong shield (shaped like a door, *thyra*) (BDAG 462). "The *thyreos* is the ancient four-cornered long shield.... The rectangular Greek shield is almost a portable wall [and] covers the whole person, which poses the hard problem of reconciling strength with lightness. The Romans take over a later form of the long shield around 340 BC and retain it until the days of Constantine, who reverts to the round or oval form" (Albrecht Oepke, *hoplon, ktl.*, TDNT 5:292-315).

on, for he knows what he is doing. Put up the shield of faith; don't let it hang useless at your side.

The Helmet of Salvation (6:17a)

"Take the helmet[20] of salvation" (6:17a)

Helmets protect the head, hence battle helmets, bicycle helmets, hard hats, and the like. Our salvation from God protects us against self-doubt and fear that God won't forgive us when we mess up. We must put on our confidence in His salvation daily and not let Satan slam us in the head with his lies. Lack of assurance of our own salvation can be devastating when we're in a spiritual battle for our lives. Get this straight. If you're not sure of your salvation, discuss this with a pastor who will give you some counsel and scripture to help you receive the assurance from God that you need to resist Satan. Remember, we are not saved by our own good works, but by grace through faith in Christ (Ephesians 2:8-9).

The Sword of the Spirit (6:17b)

"Take ... the sword of the Spirit, which is the word of God." (6:17b)

The sword,[21] too, is both offensive and defensive. We parry our enemy's blows with our sword, as well as thrust home when we see a weakness in his defense. Our sword is God's Word. When we study the Bible for its principles and truths, we can stand against Satan's lies. When Jesus was tempted during the 40 days he spent in the wilderness before beginning his ministry, he answered Satan's half-truths with Scripture (Luke 4:1-13), and so stood his ground against the Tempter. Reading the scripture often, studying it, and committing it to memory are all ways to sharpen this sword, so when we are attacked we'll know how to respond.

Q5. (Ephesians 6:15-17) Why is it important to have your "shield" up each day? In what way does the "helmet of salvation" protect you? Is the "sword of the Spirit" an offensive or defensive weapon? How do you keep it sharp and ready for the battle? http://www.joyfulheart.com/forums/index.php?showtopic=560

---

[20] *Perikephalaia*, "helmet," also 1 Thessalonians 5:8 (BDAG 802). "Greek soldiers wear bronze helmets, as do the Romans. The helmet is slung on a strap during marches and put on for battle" (Albrecht Oepke, *hoplon, ktl.*, TDNT 5:292-315).

[21] *Machaira*, "a relatively short sword or sharp instrument, sword, dagger," also used figuratively of the Word of God in Hebrews 4:12 (BDAG 622).

Pray in the Spirit (6:18)

> "And pray in the Spirit on all occasions with all kinds of prayers and requests. With this in mind, be alert and always keep on praying for all the saints." (6:18)

"Pray in the Spirit" is Paul's transition from the military analogy to a further exhortation, which we will study in the next chapter. Perhaps, though, the military analogy in our day would be, "Carry your walkie-talkie and call in when you get in trouble so we can direct firepower where you need it."

To what extent are these weapons offensive or defensive? In a very real sense they are all offensive weapons, since they allow the warrior to continue in the battle instead of being wiped out early. Part of active fighting is protecting oneself from blows so one can continue to fight.

Sometimes I've wondered if these weapons are too weak. The battle rages and all I have is a hope and a prayer and my Bible. How can I expect to find victory?

Martin Luther, who wrote that great hymn, "A Mighty Fortress Is Our God," had many well-chronicled battles with the devil. One line of this hymn is particularly telling about the devil: "One little word shall fell him." Truth will win the war with deceit and half-truth. "The pen is mightier than the sword," and God's truth is stronger than all of Satan's well-crafted lies.

We are weak in ourselves. But in God these simple weapons – truth, righteousness, the good news, faith, salvation, the Word of God, and prayer – are more than we need to fend off an attack and remain standing at the end of the day.

> "Put on the full armor of God so that you can take your stand... and having done all, to stand." (6:11, 13)

Whether we like it or not, to succeed at the Christian life we must undertake it as a conflict, a fight. That doesn't mean that we have to be negative and pessimists – only realists. There is a foe against which we must defend ourselves or live miserable, defeated lives. There is a King for whom we take the ground and claim the lives of those who are perishing. It is a fight, yes, but it is a *good* fight of faith, a *joyous* fight fought in the camaraderie of Christ and our brother and sister Christians. It is a *positive* fight, too, for if you've read the end of the book – we win! "Fight the good fight (*agōn*) of the faith," Paul tells young Timothy (1 Timothy 6:12). Then close to the time of his death, Paul recalls his own struggle – and victory in Christ:

> "I have fought the good fight, I have finished the race, I have kept the faith. Now there is in store for me the crown of righteousness, which the Lord, the righteous Judge, will

award to me on that day – and not only to me, but also to all who have longed for his appearing." (2 Timothy 2:7-8)

Prayer

Father, the more we know about the spiritual enemies arrayed against us, the more we realize we need you. I pray for faithfulness for me and for my brothers and sisters to put on the weapons daily and stand ready to fight. Help us, O Lord, for we are weak without you. Supply us continually with the strength and protection of your Spirit – and teach us to fight! In Jesus' name, we pray. Amen.

Key Verses

"For our struggle is not against flesh and blood, but against the rulers, against the authorities, against the powers of this dark world and against the spiritual forces of evil in the heavenly realms." (Ephesians 6:12)

"Therefore put on the full armor of God, so that when the day of evil comes, you may be able to stand your ground, and after you have done everything, to stand." (Ephesians 6:13)

16. Prevailing through Prayer (6:18-24)

Spiritual Warfare and Struggle

This passage is about spiritual struggle, and though we finished looking at the pieces of the armor in the previous chapter of this study, we have not yet left the subject of struggle.

> "For we struggle not against flesh and blood, but against the spiritual forces of evil in the heavenly realms" (6:12)

The word "struggle" (NIV, NRSV) and "wrestle" (KJV) in verse 12 is Greek *palē*, from Homer on down, "wrestling," a contest between two in which each endeavors to throw the other and hold him down with a hand on the neck.[1] The word is particularly used of prayer in the New Testament. The companion epistle Colossians uses the figure of an athletic event to describe intense prayer also:

We prevail by earnest prayer. Francisco de Zurbarán (1598-1664), "St. Francis in Meditation" (1635-39), oil on canvas. National Gallery, London, 162 x 137 cm.

> "... So that we may present everyone perfect in Christ. To this end I labor, struggling (*agōnizomai*) with all his energy which so powerfully works in me. I want you to know how much I am struggling (*agōn*) for you and for those in Laodicea, and for all who have not known me personally" (Colossians 1:28-2:1).

> "Epaphras ... is always wrestling (*agōnizomai*) in prayer for you, that you may stand firm in all the will of God, mature and fully assured" (Colossians 4:12).

In Romans also Paul urges his readers to:

> "... Join me in my struggle (*synagōnizaomai*) by praying to God for me...." (Romans 15:30)

---

[1] *Palē*, Thayer 474. "engagement in a challenging contest ... struggle against" (BDAG 752).

The Greek word noun *agōn* and verb *agōnizomai* were first used as "to engage in an athletic contest" and then, generally, "to struggle."[2] (We get our word "agony" from this word, though the concept of pain isn't exactly the original concept of struggling.) This word is used in Ephesians 6:12 to set the stage for the battle. The battle instruction concludes with constant prayer (6:18-20). If you've found that intercessory prayer isn't easy, that it is labor, struggle, then you share this experience with the Apostle Paul.

Pray in the Spirit (6:18)

After having taken a look at prayer as "wrestling" and "struggle," let's examine the passage at hand:

> "And pray in the Spirit on all occasions with all kinds of prayers and requests. With this
> in mind, be alert and always keep on praying for all the saints." (6:18)

Verse 18 tells us to "pray in the Spirit on all occasions with all kinds of prayers and requests." While one might argue from the 1 Corinthians 14:14-16 that praying "in the spirit" means praying in tongues, the syntax is different here. Instead of using the dative case (perhaps dative of reference) as in Corinthians, in Ephesians 6:18 Paul uses the preposition *en* ("in" or "by") to refer to the Spirit. The sense in this verse seems to be: "Pray guided by or inspired by or empowered by the Spirit." Interesting, isn't it, that even to pray effectively we need God's help.

Verse 18 tells us to "pray with all prayers and petitions." The difference between "prayers" (*proseuchē*) and a synonym, "requests" (NIV), or "supplications" (KJV, NRSV, *deēsis*) is the difference between the generic word for prayer to God, and a more specific word meaning "urgent request to meet a need, exclusively addressed to God,"[3] "seeking, asking, entreating, entreaty."[4] Notice the repetition in verse 18a of the word "all," giving emphasis to the command to pray "on *all* occasions" with "*all* kinds" of prayer. A very strong command indeed!

Q1. (Ephesians 6:18) Why is prayer vital to spiritual warfare? What does it mean to "pray in the Spirit"?

http://www.joyfulheart.com/forums/index.php?showtopic=561

---

[2] *Agōn*, BDAG 17; Ethelbert Stauffer, *agōn, ktl.*, TDNT 1:134-140.
[3] *Deēsis*, BDAG 213.
[4] *Deēsis*, Thayer 126.

Alertness in Prayer for All the Saints (6:18b)

"With this in mind, be alert and always keep on praying for all the saints." (6:18)

I don't know about you, but sometimes when I pray my mind wanders. Paul's mind must have wandered too, for his exhortation contains two commands:

1. **"Be alert"** (*agrypneō*), "to be vigilant in awareness of threatening peril, be on the alert, keep watch over something, be on guard," then "the state of being alertly concerned, care.[5]" We've found after 9/11 that after being at a state of high alert for a while, it's a natural tendency to become lax, to slough off, to go through the motions. Paul warns us that we are at war with the devil and must pray with alertness to Satan's wiles, tricks and feints (Ephesians 6:11).
2. **"Persevere"** (*proskarterēsis*), "firm persistence in an undertaking or circumstance, perseverance, patience."[6] We are to "keep on keeping on" with our praying, never flagging with diligence.

I, for one, struggle with this alertness and perseverance in prayer. Maybe you do, too. May Paul's words stimulate us to renewed diligence in prayer.

Q2. (Ephesians 6:18b) Why is alertness in prayer vital to success in spiritual warfare? How is perseverance in prayer important to success? Why do we need this exhortation?
http://www.joyfulheart.com/forums/index.php?showtopic=562

Paul Requests Prayer for Himself (6:19-20)

Having exhorted his readers to pray for "all the saints," now he requests specific prayer for himself:

"Pray also for me, that whenever I open my mouth, words may be given me so that I will fearlessly make known the mystery of the gospel, for which I am an ambassador in chains. Pray that I may declare it fearlessly, as I should." (6:19-20)

If prayer weren't really that important, Paul wouldn't urge it so strongly. But he longs for their prayers for him, knowing that the prayers of the saints empower him in his ministry. Specifically, he asks for "fearlessness" (NIV), "boldness" (KJV, NRSV),

---

[5] *Agrypneō*, BDAG 16.
[6] *Proskarterēsis*, BDAG 882.

parrēsia, "a state of boldness and confidence, courage, confidence, boldness, frankness, especially in the presence of persons of high rank."[7] Paul is in prison for preaching on the occasion of his arrest in Jerusalem (Acts 22:1-21) and on every subsequent occasion at which he appeared before those who could release him (Acts 23:1; 24:10-21, 24-25; 25:8-11; 26:1-29; 28:31). He asks for prayers that he will not slack off and compromise with fear as he awaits trial in Rome.

This same kind of courage is found in Peter and John (Acts 4:13), which causes their imprisonment. After their release, they pray:

> "Now, Lord, consider their threats and enable your servants to speak your word with great boldness (*parrēsia*)" (Acts 4:28).

If Paul must ask for prayer that he might be faithful to "fight the good fight of the faith" (1 Timothy 6:12) at his trial, how much more should we pray for one another to not only survive and hold our own, but to be fearless in the face of opposition. We must help one another through prayer! Our natural tendency is to avoid pain and persecution, but when we are going through our most difficult struggles, people watch us most closely to see whether our faith is real, or if we are just "fair-weather Christians." God give us boldness rather than a wimpy faith!

Q3. (Ephesians 6:19) Why would Paul request prayer for boldness? Why is boldness necessary in war? What is the opposite of boldness? What happens if this is our accustomed life-posture?
http://www.joyfulheart.com/forums/index.php?showtopic=563

An Ambassador in Chains (6:20a)

Paul describes himself with the curious and paradoxical phrase: "an ambassador in chains" (vs. 20). The word here is *presbeuō*, "be an ambassador or envoy, travel or work as an ambassador."[8] It refers to one who acts as an emissary, transmitting messages or negotiations, used of envoys, imperial legates, and business agents.[9]

---

[7] The basic meaning of *parrēsia* is "outspokenness, frankness, plainness." Here it has the extended meaning of "a state of boldness and confidence, courage, confidence, boldness, frankness, especially in the presence of persons of high rank" (BDAG 781-782).

[8] *Presbeuō*, BDAG 861.

[9] Günther Bornkamm, *presbys, ktl.*, TDNT 6:651-683.

Paul realizes that when he appears before the Roman emperor for trial, he will do so as the representative of his Government before the Roman court. Paul represents the King of kings and the Lord of Lords, he is the emissary of the Kingdom of God – and he must not wimp out when he is given his audience.

We, too, are ambassadors, envoys, emissaries of the Kingdom of God. Paul says to the Corinthian church, with a "we" that includes all of us:

> "We are therefore Christ's ambassadors, as though God were making his appeal through us." (2 Corinthians 5:20)

To everyone with whom our lives intersect, we are Christ's personal representatives. When we wimp out, when we neglect to identify ourselves with Christ, when we remain silent to avoid ridicule or persecution, we do the King a disservice. Jesus said, "He who receives you receives me, and he who receives me receives the one who sent me" (Matthew 10:40). What an awesome responsibility!

Q4. (Ephesians 6:20) Developing this analogy of an ambassador in a foreign land... What nation has sovereignty over the embassy and its property? Who does the ambassador represent? What responsibilities does he or she have? How do these relate to being an ambassador of Christ?
http://www.joyfulheart.com/forums/index.php?showtopic=564

Tychicus – Personal Matters (6:21-22)

> "21Tychicus, the dear brother and faithful servant in the Lord, will tell you everything, so that you also may know how I am and what I am doing. 22I am sending him to you for this very purpose, that you may know how we are, and that he may encourage you." (6:21-22)

As is customary at the conclusion of nearly all his letters, Paul moves to personal comments. He commends to them Tychicus, "the dear brother and faithful servant in the Lord" (vs. 21). Tychicus (it's fun to say – TI-ki-kis – say it) was probably from Ephesus and was Paul's traveling companion on several occasions. He brings not only the letter to the Ephesians, but also a personal report of how the Apostle is doing to "encourage" the believers there. Notice that Tychicus is not an outstanding preacher or fiery evangelist. But he is "a dear brother, a faithful minister and fellow servant in the Lord" (Colossians 4:7). You may not be outstanding, but you *can* be faithful, and you can be one who loves and is loved.

Closing Benediction (6:23-24)

Four words characterize Paul's closing benediction ("blessing") to his readers: Peace, Love, Faith, and Grace:

> "Peace to the brothers, and love with faith from God the Father and the Lord Jesus Christ. Grace to all who love our Lord Jesus Christ with an undying love." (6:23-24)

Paul began the letter with "grace and peace" and so he closes it. One of the best known verses in this great letter is probably the classic statement of what grace really is:

> "For by grace you have been saved through faith – and this not from yourselves, it is the gift of God – not by works, so that no one can boast" (2:8-9).

Sometimes in her quest for holiness, the church has de-emphasized grace in favor of a tenuous and brittle righteousness achieved by great effort of the will. But the wonder of God's work through Jesus Christ is his fully free gift of salvation – undeserved and unlimited grace – in exchange for heartfelt faith. Amazing!

However, the word used most in this benediction is love – undying love: "Love with faith from God" (6:23) and "love [for] our Lord Jesus Christ with undying love" (6:24).

May your love be undying love for the One who died for you – our Lord Jesus Christ.

Prayer

Father, in this wonderful Letter of Ephesians our eyes have been opened to many things. We pray that you would never let us take these things for granted again. I pray for my fellow comrades in arms and warriors in prayer. For my fellow ambassadors. That we might fight well, pray well, and represent you and your Kingdom well to those around us, until you call us home. In Jesus' name, I pray. Amen.

Key Verse

> "And pray in the Spirit on all occasions with all kinds of prayers and requests. With this in mind, be alert and always keep on praying for all the saints." (Ephesians 6:18)

Appendix. Participant Guide Handout Sheets

If you're working with a class or small group, feel free to duplicate the following handouts in this appendix at no additional charge. If you'd like to print 8-1/2" x 11" sheets, you can download the free Participant Guide handout sheets at: **www.jesuswalk.com/ephesians/ephesians-lesson-handouts.pdf**

Discussion Questions

You'll find 4-5 questions for each lesson. Each question may include several sub-questions. These are designed to get group members engaged in discussion of the key points of the passage. If you're running short of time, feel free to skip questions or portions of questions.

1. Spiritual Blessings in Christ (1:1-6)
2. God's Gracious Plan of Redemption (1:7-14)
3. The Greatness of Our Christian Inheritance (1:15-23)
4. From Deadness in Sin to Coming Alive in Christ (2:1-7)
5. Salvation by Grace through Faith (2:8-10)
6. Fellow Citizens with the People of God (2:11-22)
7. The Mystery, Mission, and Ministry of the Church (3:1-13)
8. Paul's Prayer and Doxology (3:14-21)
9. One Body – Unity and Diversity (4:1-10)
10. Preparation, Ministry, and Maturity (4:11-16)
11. Putting on Clean Clothes (4:17-32)
12. Imitate Your Father, Children (5:1-20)
13. Christian Husbands and Christian Wives (5:21-33)
14. Children and Parents, Employers and Employees (6:1-9)
15. Wrestling with the Enemy of Our Souls (6:10-18)
16. Prevailing through Prayer (6:18-24)

1. Spiritual Blessings in Christ (Ephesians 1:1-6)

Q1. (Ephesians 1:3) What does it mean to you to be "in Christ" – incorporated into Christ? What are the implications of this for your life?

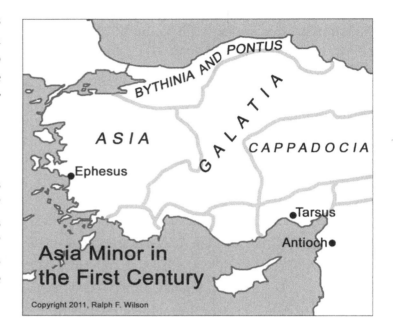

Q2. (Ephesians 1:4-5) What is scary about predestination? What is comforting? Why does Paul bring up predestination? Why do you think he is praising God for it in the "hearing" of the Ephesians?

Q3. (Ephesians 1:4) What does it mean to be "holy"? In what sense can you stand "blameless" before God?

Q4. (Ephesians 1:5-6) Why is adoption a particularly apt illustration of God's relationship with us? Why is the concept of adoption encouraging to us?

2. God's Plan of Redemption (Ephesians 1:7-14)

Q1. (Ephesians 1:7) In what sense have you been "redeemed" from slavery? What do you think your life up to now would have been like, if you hadn't been redeemed? What would your future be like without redemption, do you think?

Q2. (Ephesians 1:9-10) What is the significance that all things will be brought under one head – Christ himself? How does this relate to the Creator? What does it say about unity? *Extra Credit:* How does this verse relate to 1 Corinthians 15:24-28?

Q3. (Ephesians 1:11-12) According to verses 11 and 12, what is God's purpose for our lives? What do we need to do to fulfill this purpose? How does this purpose relate to Matthew 5:13-16?

Q4. (Ephesians 1:13-14) These verses contain two analogies: (1) seal and (2) down payment, with the balance to be paid in a lump sum at the end of the term. When does the "end of the term" occur? How do these analogies help explain how the Holy Spirit functions in our lives?

3. The Greatness of Our Christian Inheritance (Ephesians 1:15-23)

Q1. (Ephesians 1:18b) What do we Christians have to look forward to? How should this hope be a major motivation in our present-day lives? How should this hope affect our decisions and our lifestyle? How does our great hope differ from the hope of the average non-believer?

Q2. (Ephesians 1:18c) If you knew that in a few years you would inherit $10 million, would it affect your life now? How should our expectation of an inheritance in God's presence temper our present-day concerns? Since this inheritance will be shared with "the saints" – our Christian family – how should that affect our fellowship with them?

Q3. (Ephesians 1:18d) Why are we powerless sometimes? Is it an inadequacy with the source or with our faith? Why do some congregations and movements produce disciples with miracle-believing faith and others produce disciples with wimpy faith? How can this be changed?

Q4. (Ephesians 1:20-22) Why do we so often take a "pass" when it comes to spiritual warfare? Why is Christ's exaltation, demonstration of complete victory, and superior rank over all spiritual powers important enough for Paul to mention it to his readers? Why do we tend to feel powerless in the face of spiritual enemies? What was Paul assuring the Ephesians of? What does this encourage us to do?

Q5. (Ephesians 1:22-23) When we neglect to be an active part of a local congregation, what particular blessings do we miss out on according to Paul in this verse? How do we, by our absence, withhold this blessing from others?

4. From Deadness in Sin to Coming Alive in Christ (Ephesians 2:1-7)

Q1. (Ephesians 2:1-3) In what sense are our non-believing friends, neighbors, and relatives "dead"? What's the difference between us and them? If we really believed that they were "dead" and subject to God's "wrath," what would we do?

Q2. (Ephesians 2:1-3) Few people would knowingly follow Satan. How can people unwittingly follow Satan? In what sense are we responsible for unwitting rebellion against God? How can God, in all fairness, blame us?

Q3. (Ephesians 1:4-5) In verses 4 and 5, which words describe God's motivation and character? Which verbs describe what has happened to us in Christ?

Q4. (Ephesians 2:6) What does it mean that we are seated with Christ in "the heavenly realms"? What does this say about God's grace? What does this say about our spiritual authority? How should this knowledge affect our prayers and our boldness?

5. Salvation By Grace Through Faith (Ephesians 2:8-10)

Q1. Why is it so hard for us to understand grace? What commonly held life principle does it demolish? Translate the word "grace" into language a 10-year-old child would understand.

Q2. "Saved" has become Christian jargon. How can you "translate" this word into modern speech so people can understand what it really means and why they need it?

Q3. According to Ephesians 2:10, what were we created to do? Why? (Matthew 5:16) What is the difference between these works and the works Paul discredits in verse 9?

Q4. What exactly is faith? Can we take credit for having it? Can we be condemned for lacking it? Define "faith" in terms a 10-year-old could understand.

6. Fellow Citizens with the People of God (Ephesians 2:11-22)

Q1. (Ephesians 2:11-12) Why does being out of touch with what it means to be "lost" impede our willingness to witness? In your own words, what is the spiritual condition of a friend or co-worker who doesn't know Christ?

Q2. (Ephesians 2:14-15) In what sense did Jesus as Messiah "fulfill" the Mosaic Law? What is the significance of that for Jewish people? For us Gentiles?

Q3. (Ephesians 2:17) What does it mean to have "access to the Father"? In what way does the Holy Spirit facilitate this access? In what way does Jesus enable this access?

Q4. (Ephesians 2:22) What is the significance that your congregation was made to be "a dwelling place for God in the Spirit"? What hinders that from being fully experienced? What can you do to help that become more fully experienced and appreciated?

7. The Mystery, Mission, and Ministry of the Church (Ephesians 3:1-13)

Q1. (Ephesians 3:2-5) Why is God's revelation to "his holy apostles and prophets" our authority for faith and practice? What is the danger of minimizing or straying from that revelation? What is the danger of superseding that revelation? What is the danger of denying that God reveals himself to us and to his church today?

Q2. (Ephesians 3:6) Just what is the "mystery" that Paul is talking about? Why was it important to the Gentile Christians in Paul's day?

Q3. (Ephesians 3:7-9) Why is Paul so careful to be humble about his call and apostleship? How can his example help us remain as humble servants?

Q4. What does Ephesians 3:12 teach us about the manner of approaching God? What happens if we try to pray without these qualities?

8. Paul's Prayer and Doxology (Ephesians 3:14-21)

Q1. (Ephesians 3:16-17) Do the concepts of (a) strengthened by the Spirit in the inner person, and (b) Christ dwelling in our hearts say the same thing, or are they separate and distinct ideas? What do you think?

Q2. (3:18-19) What kinds of things prevent us from comprehending the far reaches of Christ's love? What happens in the way we live when we do comprehend, know, and experience this love? What would be different about your life if you could grasp this?

Q3. (Ephesians 3:16, 19) What does it mean to be "filled with the Spirit" (verse 16)? Is this a one-time experience or a continual reality? What can we do to be filled with the Spirit? Is it different or the same as being "filled with all the fullness of God" (verse 19)?

Q4. (Ephesians 3:21) What might be different in your own congregation if bringing glory to God were considered the very most important function of the church? What would be different in your life if bringing God glory was your most important job, bar none?

9. One Body – Unity and Diversity (Ephesians 4:1-10)

Q1. (Ephesians 4:1) According to verse 1, what is the standard of our behavior? What is the "calling" to which God has called us?

Q2. (Ephesians 4:2) Why are patience and humility so important to preserving unity? What happens to the reputation of Jesus Christ when we have right doctrine along with a sense of arrogance towards those who disagree with us? How are we to be both "gentle" and to "fight the good fight of faith"?

Q3. (Ephesians 4:3) How much energy must we expend on Christian unity? What is "the bond of peace"? How do we strike at peace when we are intent on argument and dissension?

Q4. (Ephesians 4:7-10) Who gives spiritual gifts? Can our "natural" talents be related to our "spiritual" gifts? How? What is the difference between a natural God-given talent and a spiritual gift?

10. Preparation, Ministry, and Maturity (Ephesians 4:11-16)

Q1. (Ephesians 4:11) If there were apostles today, why kind of function might they have? What needs do our congregations and regional groupings of churches have that an apostle might meet? How might we detect false apostles? (2 Corinthians 11:13; Revelation 2:2)

Q2. (Ephesians 4:11) How can we stir up the gift of evangelism among members of our congregations? What might be the earmarks of a person with this gift? How can we encourage and stimulate the Spirit-gifted evangelists in our midst?

Q3. (Ephesians 4:11) How could a person have the spiritual gift of pastor or teacher without having an official position in a church? What must a church do if its "senior pastor" doesn't have the spiritual gift of pastor? Who gives these gifts?

Q4. (Ephesians 4:12) What's wrong with the old model of the minister or pastor being the main worker in the Church? How does it hinder people in the congregation? How does it hurt the community? What is the purpose of pastors and teachers?

Christ gave apostles, prophets, evangelists, pastors, and teachers
> *In order to* (*pros*) prepare and equip God's people (12a)
> *For* (*eis*) works of service (*diakonia*), (12b)
> *and for* (*eis*) building up the body of Christ (12c)
> *So that* we may reach unity in the faith (13a) *and* grow into the full maturity of Christ
> (Ephesians 4:13b - 16)

11. Putting on Clean Clothes (Ephesians 4:17-32)

Q1. (Ephesians 4:17-19) Using Ephesians 4:17-19 as a basis, how would you describe (in your own words), the secular, non-Christian mindset of our age? Why are we tempted to conform to its values?

Q2. (Ephesians 4:26-27). Why did God give us the emotion of anger, do you think? How can anger be dangerous? How can we keep from sinning when we are angry? Is anger itself sin?

Q3. (Ephesians 4:29-32) What kind of "unwholesome talk" is common among us Christians? What three guidelines does Paul give us to measure the value of what we say? What is slander? How common is it among Christians? How can we prevent it?

Q4. (Ephesians 4:32) Why is it so difficult to forgive those who hurt us? According to Ephesians 4:32, who is our example of forgiveness? What heart attitudes toward people are evidence of a forgiving spirit, according to verse 32a?

12. Imitate Your Father, Children (Ephesians 5:1-20)

Q1. (Ephesians 5:2-3) Why does Paul warn so strongly against sexual sin? Is sexuality part of our spiritual life or can it be (should it be) partitioned from our spiritual life?

Q2. (Ephesians 5:15-16) Why does Paul exhort us to make the most of every opportunity? Why do we resist that? What must happen in our lives so we can be ready for the opportunity?

Q3. (Ephesians 5:17-18) What is the primary temptation involved with drugs and alcohol? How can drug or alcohol use substitute for the "high" of the Spirit? How can being filled with the Spirit help us fend off the temptations of drugs and alcohol?

Q4. (Ephesians 5:19-20) What kind of attitude should underlie our corporate singing? How is corporate singing designed to help us singers? How is it designed to worship God? How does singing in your own daily life help you worship?

13. Christian Husbands and Christian Wives (Ephesians 5:21-33)

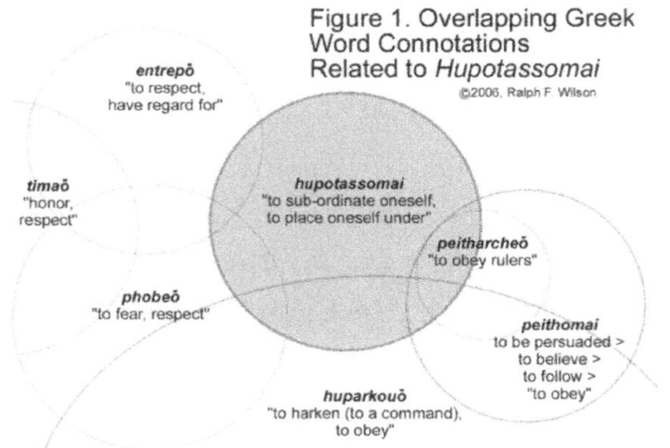

Q1. (Ephesians 5:22-24) Why should a wife submit to her husband? According to these verses, to what degree is a wife required to submit to a husband who is not a Christian or who is a carnal Christian? Does submission mean a wife doesn't verbally disagree? What if there's a conflict with the wife's conscience?

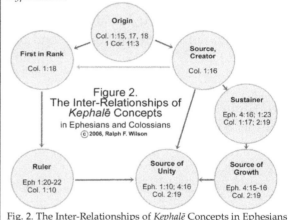

Fig. 1. Overlapping Greek Word Connotations Related to *Hypotassomai*.

Q2. (Ephesians 5:25-30) Does being head of the wife involve being "boss"? Why or why not? What does being "head" require of a husband? What is the example husbands are to follow in headship?

Q3. (Ephesians 5:28) In what sense is a husband's care for his wife's needs just common sense in taking care of his own needs? What is the principle from Genesis 2:24 that underlies this?

Fig. 2. The Inter-Relationships of *Kephalē* Concepts in Ephesians and Colossians.

Q4. (Ephesians 5:32) In what sense is Christ our Husband as individuals? As a church? What are the implications of this for our lives? What does this say about Christ's responsibilities towards us?

14. Children and Parents, Employers and Employees (Ephesians 6:1-9)

Q1. (Ephesians 6:1-3) What kind of obedience and honor is appropriate for adult children to show towards their parents? What might be the exceptions? How do respect and forgiveness figure in this relationship?

Q2. (Ephesians 6:4) What kind of behavior by fathers (or mothers, for that matter) can embitter or cause a child to lose heart? What do you think the "training and instruction of the Lord" involves?

Q3. (Ephesians 6:5-8) What are the characteristics called for in a truly Christian employee, according to Ephesians 6:5-8? How can these attitudes help us in difficult work situations?

Q4. (Ephesians 6:9) How should Christian employers conduct themselves towards their employees? How should church boards conduct themselves towards church employees? How do you determine a just wage – not merely the one you think you can afford?

15. Wrestling with the Enemy of Our Souls (Ephesians 6:10-18)

Q1. (Ephesians 6:11-13) Why is it difficult to believe in the devil and demons in our day? How does their existence help explain the struggle humans face on earth? With all their power, how do we stand a chance? Did "the devil make me do it"? What kinds of things *can't* we blame on the demonic?

Q2. (Ephesians 6:13) What is difficult about standing our ground in today's world? In what way can standing our ground be considered victory? Why are the saints in Revelation 12:11 considered victorious over the devil? How did they stand their ground?

Q3. (Ephesians 6:14) Why are such simple things as truth and personal holiness such powerful armament? Are they defensive or offensive weapons?

Q4. (Ephesians 6:15) What would be the characteristic of a person who *didn't* have his feet ready to run with the Gospel? How does heart preparation make you more ready to share the Good News with those around you? How does this help defeat the dominion of darkness?

Q5. (Ephesians 6:15-17) Why is it important to have your "shield" up each day? In what way does the "helmet of salvation" protect you? Is the "sword of the Spirit" an offensive or defensive weapon? How do you keep it sharp and ready for the battle?

16. Prevailing through Prayer (Ephesians 6:18-24)

Q1. (Ephesians 6:18) Why is prayer vital to spiritual warfare? What does it mean to "pray in the Spirit"?

Q2. (Ephesians 6:18b) Why is alertness in prayer vital to success in spiritual warfare? How is perseverance in prayer important to success? Why do we need this exhortation?

Q3. (Ephesians 6:19) Why would Paul request prayer for boldness? Why is boldness necessary in war? What is the opposite of boldness? What happens if this is our accustomed life-posture?

Q4. (Ephesians 6:20) Developing this analogy of an ambassador in a foreign land... What nation has sovereignty over the embassy and its property? Who does the ambassador represent? What responsibilities does he or she have? How do these relate to being an ambassador of Christ?